AF787615

Academic Foundation

Financial Economics of
Bonus Shares

Financial Economics of Bonus Shares

IMPLICATIONS FOR THE VALUE OF THE FIRM

S. Narasimha Sarma

ACADEMIC FOUNDATION

24-A, Sriram Road, Civil Lines, Delhi - 110 054. (India)

Phone : 233730, 232966, 2911852

Published in 1993 by
ACADEMIC FOUNDATION
24 - A, Sriram Road, Civil Lines, Delhi - 110 054.
Tel : 232966, 233730, 2911852.

FINANCIAL ECONOMICS OF BONUS SHARES
S. Narasimha Sarma
ISBN 81-7188-078-9

Laser-Typeset by
COMPRINT INDIA, Delhi

Financial Economics
of
Bonus Shares

IMPLICATIONS FOR THE VALUE OF THE FIRM

S. Narasimha Sarma

ACADEMIC FOUNDATION

24-A, Sriram Road, Civil Lines, Delhi - 110 054. (India)
Phone : 233730, 232966, 2911852

Published in 1993 by
ACADEMIC FOUNDATION
24 - A, Sriram Road, Civil Lines, Delhi - 110 054.
Tel : 232966, 233730, 2911852.

FINANCIAL ECONOMICS OF BONUS SHARES
S. Narasimha Sarma
ISBN 81-7188-078-9

Laser-Typeset by
COMPRINT INDIA, Delhi

TO MY MOTHER

Late Srimati Rajya Lakshmi

Contents

Foreword

THE news of a bonus issue is generally a thriller. It is greeted with cheers by the market. A very widely prevalent belief is that bonus *per se* is of value and has a direct positive influence on share prices. In fact, market participants attempt to ferret out information about a bonus-issue-in-the-offing. They rely even upon guesses, rumours, and unfiltered leakages of inside information. All this effort is supposed to send convulsions in prices and brace up the possibility of speculative gains for the better-informed or for better predictors.

Theoretical discussions have gone deeper behind the market psyche built around bonus expectations. It is plain to agree with the Financial Accountant that a bonus issue *per se* does not alter the ownership interest of equity-holders. In fact, the net-worth pie gets divided into smaller pieces in view of the number of shares having been increased in proportion to the rate of bonus issue. Thus, one might argue that the intrinsic worth or book value remains the same as before the issue of bonus shares and may even decline on a per share basis. Then, what it is that the market is reckoning around ? Why do market prices change in anticipation of bonus? Is bonus a fundamental factor ?

These questions seem to be evoking an explanation to the possibility of some market irrationality being at work. One would, of course, stress that the market as a whole cannot be wrong. Bonus produces a favourable impact all round.

The present research arose out of a review of such notions. Effort has been made to explore the relationship between bonus issues and share prices. Two approaches have been tried. In one of them, bonus has been treated as an 'event' like any other event, namely, dividend, rights issue, earnings announcement, etc. And, established 'event-time' methodology has been used to uncover the relationship. The announcement date is the base date and the 'event-time' has been extended on either side of the base date. The pre-base-date time records price impacts of early guesses and later unconfirmed information trickles. The post-base-date period records the duration of the price impact or the duration and extent of price correction. One would expect a theoretical correction equivalent to the factor 1/1+r where 'r' is the bonus ratio. The actual correction may, in fact, not be equal to the theoretical correction. If actual correction lags behind the theoretical (or expected) correction, one might infer that some known (or unknown) fundamental factor is operating to prevent the full-scale regression of prices to the pre-bonus level. Contrarywise, an adverse force is pulling the market abruptly down and leads to the state of over-correction.

A close-shaven view of the price-impact under an event-time methodology could be focussed by restricting the event-time on either side of the base-data, say, a week before and a weak after. But since, in imperfect and discontinuous markets as the Indian markets in general are, such an effort may be more frustrating than insightful. It may well be the case that the number of trading days within a total band of fifteen days with base date being centred may be quite a small number. Also, the scrip may not be a super-active one and there may not be any quotations for most of the time. Another important consideration is the aggregate procedural time-span that elapses between the preparation of the internal spread-sheet and the final issue of scrips. The present study has used this broadened time-span for analysing the price-impact.

The other approach is multiple regression analysis using 'bonus issue' as one of the independent variables. This is in the usual run of the mill style. The usual tests of significance with confidence intervals have been undertaken and regression runs obtained for time-series data extending over a period of ten years.

It is interesting to observe that both the methodologies unmistakably point up to the irrelevance of bonus shares as influencers of share prices. Theoretically speaking, this is not an unusual conclusion. All early pioneering studies astonished market players with similar findings.

If one ponders over the economic logic emerging from the empirical tests in the present study and several others in the past, the intermediating variable that embodies the basic relationship between share price and bonus shares gets immediately manifest.

It is common knowledge that the market discounts the available and past information in current prices. Changes from this point onward would have to be premised on expected events. Now, a bonus issue today (with a formation period extending over the past several weeks) triggers off a series of expectations and all of them are focussed on the quantum of dividend per share on an adjusted basis (i.e., pre-bonus position). For example, Maharashtra Scooters which gave a 1:1 bonus during 1989-90 announced a 25 per cent dividend for 1990-91 which, on an adjusted basis, works out to 50 per cent and is 10 percentage points more than the pre-bonus dividend rate of 40 percent for 1989-90. The share price ruled around Rs. 230/- before the Board meeting convened on May 8, 1991 for considering accounts and declaring a dividend and it came down to Rs. 217/- on May 9, 1991 at the BSE. The fall in the price may be attributed to the dividend announcement falling short of market expectations. But since the adjusted dividend is larger than the previous year, it gives rise to expectations of a brighter future and may hold the price around Rs. 215/- for some time.

Another interesting example from recent corporate performance reports is again from the same industry, viz., two wheeler but pertaining to the market leader and a star performer. The 10-rupee share of Bajaj Auto was quoted on BSE at Rs. 655/- on May 13, 1991. The track-record of the company includes a one-for-one bonus in 1987-88 and a dividend of 110 per cent for the ninth-month period (on an adjusted basis) ending March 31, 1990. The equity dividend for 1990-91 has been slashed down to 100 per cent in view of reduced profitability and the share price was quoted at Rs. 640/- on May 14, 1991, i.e. making a decline of Rs. 15/- in just one day The Board's decision to reduce dividend has been capitalised by the market. However, the reserves of the company amount to Rs. 298.50 crores as against a paid up capital of Rs. 18.81 crores. This has generated hopes of another liberal bonus issue with further larger dividend expectations in 1991-92. Directors are to take a decision with regard to the bonus sometime in June. The share price will again move in anticipation of a bonus and subsequent dividend escalations.

It would, thus, be seen that the real fundamental factor behind price movements is the dividend expectation which, inter alia, may be influenced by the current rate and quantum of bonus issue.

Dr. Sarma's present work incorporates these market intonations which he gleaned through a preliminary short survey. The respondents were company-level finance officials and eminent brokers and other market participants.

Collection of daily price quotations for a long period of over one year has indeed, been an uphill task but the researcher performed it assiduously.

The structure of the study has primarily emerged out of the pioneering work done by Brown and Warner (Using Daily Stock Returns-The Case of Event Studies: Journal of Financial Economics 14 (1985) 3-31. North Holland). As in all such studies, Dr. Sarma has used the expected theoretical correction as a basis for measuring deviations of post-ex-date prices. (Explained in detail, in the text material or Chapter 1).

I am given to understand that the study claims neither absolute originality nor finality. This is though the stark reality, the effort made by Dr. Sarma does provide new insights in developing a theoretical backdrop for the valuation of bonus shares in the Indian market and legal background. Also, the work provoking as it does quite a few controversies must encourage further research in the area with a fundamentalist fervour. I am, indeed, very happy to write these lines as foreword. Dr. Sarma, in my view, deserves sincere congratulations for his painstaking study. I wish the work a great success in its published format.

— Prof. Braj Kishor

DEAN, FACULTY OF COMMERCE
OSMANIA UNIVERSITY, HYDERABAD

Preface

THE focus of this study is on analysing if bonus shares have any causative implications on the changes in share prices. In addition, it includes an analysis of the characteristic features of bonus issues made by the Indian private corporate sector during 1977-88 and the post-bonus dividend changes.

That the Indian corporate sector relatively favoured capitalisation of reserves in high ratios; that an overwhelming majority of the bonus issues were associated with an increased dividend quantum and that bonus shares 'per se' are not seen as of any value by the market, emerge as important findings of this study.

These findings, of course, are subject to certain qualifications and exceptions which are discussed in the study. Further, these findings are based on the data relating to the period 1977-78. Nevertheless, these findings are in broad conformity with that of other empirical studies in India and abroad.

I am heavily indebted to Prof. Braj Kishor, Dean, Faculty of Commerce, Osmania University, Hyderabad, under whose supervision this work has been done. But for his guidance, encouragement and support, not only as supervisor but also as a philosopher friend, the work would have not been just possible.

I owe a debt of gratidude to Prof. Lamoureux, Department of Finance, College of Business Administration, Louisiana State University, USA, whose work originally inspired me to undertake this study, for very promptly providing the documentation on the 'Event-Time' methodology. I am also greatly indebted to Prof. Peter C. Eisemann, Georgia State University, Atlanta, USA who, on request, promptly spared a copy of his article on 'Stock Dividends: Managements' View'.

I am greatful to Mr. S. Thirumalai, Vice-President [Finance] and Company Secretary, VST Industries Ltd., Mr. P. Raghavendra Rao, Vice-President [Finance], IDL Chemicals Ltd., Mr. G.D. Sultania, Vice-President [Finance], Hyderabad Industries Ltd., Mr. Balaji, Vice-President [Finance], Bhadrachalam Papers Boards Ltd., Mr.

Kumara Swamy. Company Secretary, Coromandal Fertilisers, Mr. A.P. Rao, Managing Director, Standard Equity Fund Ltd., and Mr. Laxman Rao Shankpal, Secretary, Hyderabad Stock Exchange Ltd., of Hyderabad and Mr. V.P. Parameswaran, Finance Controller, Associated Cement Co. Ltd., Mr. Babubhai Shah, Vice President [Finance], Standard Mill Co. Ltd., Nalin. N. Shah, Secretary, Indian Dye Stuff Industries Ltd., and Mr. M.V. Patwardhan, Vice-President, National Organic Chemical Industries Ltd., of Bombay with whom I had fruitful discussions and whose thought provoking views have enriched my understanding of the subject and also contributed to the methodology of this study.

I appreciate the help extended by Dr. M.R. Mayya, Executive Director, Bombay Stock Exchange, who kindly permitted to gather information from the records of the Exchange and also by Mr. Dinanath S. Sarmalker who cheerfully took the burden of identifying the files and providing the information required regarding the 'announcement dates'. I am thankful to Dr. V.A. Avadhani, Director, Training Institute, Bombay Stock Exchange who provided supporting documentation and to Mr. Ramesh, Statistics and Computer Data Cell, Bombay Stock Exchange, who gave a copy of Bombay Stock Exchange Sensitivity Index booklet.

I am very much pleased and encouraged by a very sincere response to my 'Information Schedule' by executives of 69 companies. I am beholden to them and to their assistants.

I have used the library and documentation facilities available at the Institute of Public Enterprises, The Administrative Staff College of India, The National Institute for Small Industries Extension and Training, Hyderabad Stock Exchange and Osmania University. I am obliged to the librarians of these institutes, particularly, Mr. Sarma, Ms. Puspa, and Ms. Sujata Rao of IPE, Dr. Sudarshanam Padam of ASCI, Mr. Laxman Rao Shankpal of HSE Ltd., Mr. Ram Das, Mr. Anjaiah, Miss. Nazima, and Mr. Sastry of OU for their ready service.

My senior colleagues in the department, Prof. Laxmi Narain, Prof. E.G. Parameshwaran, Prof. B. Govardhan Reddy, Dr. Ch. Shyam Sunder, Dr. P. Maruthi Ram, Dr. C. Madhusudana Reddy, Dr. S.S. Murthy, and Mr. K. Narendra Nath have continually encouraged and helped in various ways in my pursuit. I remain thankful for their acts of kindness.

I am the greatest beneficiery of the newly installed computer facility in our department which helped to expedite the work. I am indeed obliged to Miss. K.C. Chandrika, Programmer, and to Dr. Pannalal, Reader and In-Charge, Computer Center, Department of Business Management for their unhesitating co-operation.

Editors or Chartered Secretary and ASCI Journal of Management have encouraged me by publishing "Bonus Shares — Legal underpinings" and Bonus Shares - Divident charges in other Journals respectively. I am indeed thankful to them for permitting me to secure the material in other book.

Thanks are due to the University Grants Commission for making funds available for this study.

I have no words to express my gratitude to the kind hearted couple, Prof. S.R. Sarma, my paternal uncle and his wife Mrs. S.R. Rajeswary who brought me up in life with compassion and unmindful of sacrifices involved. I pity myself for my inability to express gratitude to my grand mother, late Mrs. Durgamba, who toiled too hard to bring me up in life. I must go on record the unfaltered cheerful support extended by my wife, Mrs. S.S. Laskshmi in this endeavour. I must also recall the playful prattle of my kids, baby Virajita and master Tejaswy, around my working table compelling to improve my ability to concentrate.

— ***S.N. Sarma***

DEPARTMENT OF BUSINESS MANAGEMENT
OSMANIA UNIVERSITY, HYDERABAD

List of Tables

I

Introduction

I. Problem

This study investigates and analyses if bonus shares issued by the Indian Corporate Sector during 1977-88 provided a real gain to the investors. The underlying debate centers around the broad theme whether bonus shares are of any investment value to the shareholders.

There is unanimity in opinion both among the practitioners and theoreticians that the value of the firm largely depends on the future expected cash flows. Any changes in the amount and pattern of expected net cash flow are likely to convey corresponding changes in the value of the firm. A number of studies have identified changes in cash dividends and capital structure[1] as signals for possible changes in the expected cash flows leading to changes in the value of the firm. Lintner[2] and Michaelsen [3] have demonstrated that once the dividends have been increased, large firms show great reluctance to reduce them except under the most extreme conditions. Directors have been found to hedge against such possibilities of dividend cuts by practicing considerable conservatism in deciding for an increase in dividends in the first instance. They consented to a raise in the dividend rate only when they have ensured that the jacked up rate would be sustained for some future years at least. It is interesting to observe events like issue of bonus shares or sub-division of shares (split into units of lower denomination) have been considered to be variables having no influence on expected future cash flows and hence, neutral to the value of the firm. The empirical evidence, of course, is not conclusive. Empirical evidence both confirming and refuting the direct positive association between the occurrence of such events and value of the firm has been reported.

The present chapter states the problem as given above in this section and defines the objectives of this study in section two. The third section of the chapter describes the scope of the study and the section that follows provides a summary of the empirical work having a direct and indirect bearing on the relationship between bonus shares and the share prices. The fifth section generates and defines the hypothesis along with the assumptions that comprise the research base for the present study. The methodology for the investigation has been outlined in the sixth section and the last section presents the total chapter plan for the entire investigation.

II. Objectives

The objectives of this study can be delineated as follows:

1. To understand the environment to issue bonus shares in India specifically by identifying the characteristic features of bonus issues made by the Indian Companies over the period of study.

2. To estimate the extent to which bonus issues are accompanied and/or followed by an 'undiluted dividend' distribution[4].

3. To make an attempt to suggest the dividend and bonus effects on the market valuation of equity shares.

III. Scope of the Study

Sample Companies

The present study examines the bonus issues made by public limited companies listed on the Bombay Stock Exchange [BSE] which is the premier stock market of the country and which accounts for a very predominant chunk of around 49% of the aggreagate turnover of major stock exchanges in the country[5]. The sample companies are either medium or large sized[6]. Public Limited Companies which announced at least one bonus issue between January 1, 1977 and March 31, 1988 have been included. To analyse the exclusive price consequences of bonus announcement, the bonus issues included for that purpose are such that they are not associated with any concurrent or simultaneous dividend announcement. Exclusion of bonus issues announced after March 31, 1988 is done because, post-bonus announcement price effect could not be observed and analysed adequately. The issues some times appearing like scrips sans consideration, which in fact are not analogous to bonus shares, have been excluded from this study to avoid the possibility of misinterpretation[7]. All the sample companies whether domestic or multi-nationals are those whose registered office is located in India and which are at the same time listed on the Bombay Stock Exchange.

Sample Period

This study covers bonus issues announced during a period of 12 years from 1977 to 1988[8]. The choice of this period is primarily influenced by the corporate investment behaviour acquiring a new surge after a series of set backs since the commencement of fourth five year plan and during the plan holiday period. It may be mentioned that the dividend freeze coming in the wake of the Dividend Restriction Ordinance, 1974 introduced an abnormal situation in the market. It was thought that the study period should be such as is not influenced by abnormal events of this kind. What provides relevance to such events is the fact that a bonus issue decision of a company is primarily an earnings retention decision which in turn is taken when the companies have no substantial investment programmes. It is not difficult to see set backs to company level investments when the economy faces a recession or a deceleration of investment activity. The entire period beginning with mid-sixties and up to mid-seventies was characterised by such a situation[9] and, therefore, has been excluded. Moreover, the first quarter of the year 1988 would provide an update on the emerging market pattern of bonus issues and consequential share valuation.

The notable events during the period selected for this study have been the announcement of concessions in the area of long term capital gains and the modifications of the specific bonus guidelines in August, 1981. The Dividend Restriction Ordinance was repealed during 1975 and its spill over effect was seen to be subsiding roughly by 1976. Therefore, bonus issues made after 1976 have been considered for the purpose of this study.

IV. Review of Literature

Existing literature on bonus share valuation consists two broad groups of empirical evidences: 1. those which observe a direct positive relationship between bonus shares and value of the firm and 2. those which find this relationship to be weak or non-existent.

Some studies have been in the nature of opinion surveys and have been incorporated to suggest the basic relationship between bonus shares and value of the firm.

A Non-Evident Relationship

Barker's study[10] may be considered as one of the pioneering attempts in exploring the market implications of stock dividends[11]. He examined two broad aspects in this context. The first aspect related to price effect of stock dividends and the second analysed the ownership effects of such dividends. It was Barker who has clearly listed out the various arguments in support of issuing stock dividends by the USA corporations. He stated:

> "Opinions of financial analysts differ widely and strongly. Some believe that small stock dividends lead to increases in market price by broadening the shareownership, while some feel they bring about

real value enhancement for shareowners without any such rise. Others emphasize that stock dividends offer tax benefits to higher income bracket investors because they are not generally treated as income for tax purposes. Still others feel that although stock dividends may have no apparent effect on the market value of the investment, they are useful in conserving corporate cash and are therefore an inexpensive way to raise capital for expansion. A final school of thought claims that stock dividends, like stock splits, merely cut the same loaf of bread in a larger number of necessary thinner slices."

And it is he, who has provided an unequivocal empirical evidence to conclude that:

Despite strong opinion to the contrary, however, stock dividends alone, whether large or small, produce no lasting gains in market price for widely held stock on national exchanges. They are not a means of avoiding double taxation of dividends, nor are they customarily employed to conserve cash. Moreover, plans for regularised issuance of stock dividends are extremely difficult to carry out, because of the fluctuating market price limitation on earned surplus transfers imposed by accounting requirements. Stock dividends are also more expensive to issue than stock spolit distributions and, all things considered, an inconvenience to shareholders."

Barker studied the price implications of the stock dividends by considering them under three following situations: 1. when accompanied by cash dividend increases, 2. when accompanied by no such increases or with actual decline in cash dividends and 3. when the cash dividends were omitted altogether. Barker centered his price and stock dividend data on the ex-stock dividend date and moved six months back from this date for his base period and moved forward by another six months to reach the final time point for comparison. Thus, his first set of comparison was between the base date (six months prior) and the ex-stock dividend date and his second comparison was between the ex-stock dividend date and the final time point (six months after). The total period of study spanning over the 12 months afforded an opportunity for analysing the beginning of stock dividend effect and the final shaping of such effects. This approach enabled Barker to avoid extraneous elements or the chaotic effect of a second, overlapping stock dividend. His sample consisted of 224 issues with a stock dividend rate of 5% or more. His findings with regard to price effects are summarised in Table-1.1 given.

Table - 1.1
Price Effect of Stock Dividends

	Price at selected date (%)		
	6 months prior to Ex-Date	At Ex-Date	6 months after Ex-Date
Accompanied by Cash Dividend increases:	100	109	108
No Cash Dividend Increases:	100	99	88

It will be seen from Table-1.1 that the price index number moved up from 100 on the base date to 109 on the ex-date and marginally came down to 108 six months after the ex-date in the case of stock dividend issues accompanied by cash dividend increases. In contrast, the index number of share prices came down by 1% to 99 on ex-date and recorded a net decline of 12% to 88 six months after the ex-date in comparison with base date in the case of stock dividends not accompanied by cash dividend increases. Barker found that to achieve an 8% average real gain in price (between the base date and the date six months after ex-date) companies paid an additional dividend of 17% in terms of adjusted cash dividend per share. From this he concluded that what really influenced the price increase was not the stock dividend but a significant increase in cash dividend as a result of which the firms' competitive cash dividend paying capacity emerges as the most significant determinant of lasting price gain.

An interesting feature that underlined Barker's study is that even though the price effects of stock dividend are very weak, the ownership effects are quite significant. By lowering the price at which shares are traded and then bringing them within a more popular trading range stock dividends served to broaden the ownership base of issuing corporations. Table-1.2 summarises the result relating to his study on ownership changes due to stock dividend issues.

Table - 1.2
Effects of Stock Dividend on Share Ownership

	% increase in share ownership 1950-53
Stock dividend of 25% or more	30
Stock dividend of 5-25%	17
All stock dividends	25
No stock dividend or split	5

It is obvious from Table - 1.2 that the large stock dividends resulted in the largest percentage increase in share ownership. On an average the use of stock dividends increased shareholders by 25%. The increase in ownership of those companies having no stock dividends or splits was just 5%. Further, the degree of increase in ownership increased with the size of stock dividend.

Though Barker made a pioneering attempt to empirically test the implications of stock dividend he has not addressed his study to the issue relating to the speed of adjustment of share price to the new information implicit in stock dividend issues. Secondly, the semi strong form of the Efficient Market Hypothesis expects the market to react to new information around the announcement date rather than the ex-date. Therefore, the conclusions based on ex-date reaction may not suggest very valid market response pattern to the information content of stock dividends. Finally, Barker's study does not also reflect that there is often a strong but short lived price run up during the first few days after news of stock dividend reaches the public particularly when the dividend is a special, non-periodic one not expected by an average investor.

Later, many authors and researchers have agreed with the findings of Barker. For example Cohen and Zinberg[12] said:

> "There is considerable statistical evidence to suggest that favourable price response is not due to the stock dividend *per se*, but rather to the fact that the cash dividend per share is usually maintained on the greater number of shares so that the stock dividend really means an effective increase in the cash dividend."

Van Horne[13] states as follows:

> "Stock dividend can also be a thing of value to the investors if the company maintains the same cash dividend per share after the stock dividend as before... In this case, a stock dividend increases his total cash dividends. Whether this increase in cash dividend has a positive effect upon shareholder wealth will depend upon the trade off between current dividends and retained earnings... Clearly, the stock dividends in this case represents a decision by the firm to increase the amount of cash dividend."

In the Indian context Gupta[14] made a pioneering study on the implications of issuing bonus shares. He covered the characteristic features of bonus issues of Indian companies, the dividend effect of bonus issues and the share price changes associated with bonus issues in his study. His analysis covered the bonus issues of 1948-71. His conclusions were that the great majority of the bonus issues in India are in relatively high ratio of 20% and above and are made by companies at irregular intervals without any consistent policy; that the bonus issues by Indian companies are more in the nature of stock splits than stock dividends because a significant proportion of such issues are not followed by any increase in the quantum of dividend distribution and in remaining cases the dividend increase is ordinarily less in proportion to the bonus issues; and that whereas the immediate price rise was directly related to bonus ratios the price change after a year showed no such relationship.

An interesting observation made by Gupta pertains to stock splits and stock dividends. He appears to hold the view that bonus issues by Indian companies are more in the nature of 'stock splits' than 'stock dividends' of USA corporations. The reasoning for a more proximate analogy of Indian bonus shares with the USA's Stock Split is premised on his observed view that a significant proportion of such issues in India are not followed by any increase in the quantum of dividend distribution or dividend increase is ordinarily less than in proportion to bonus ratio[15].

Gupta makes further observation that the share market considers bonus shares with a 'mythical reverence, not quite justified by the facts'[16]. This should be considered appropriate if bonus does not affect future dividends from the companies' point of view or shareholders' point of view. In fact, there is a school of thought which considers even dividends to be irrelevant as far as their effect on share price is concerned[17]. Research in India addressed to this theme finds such a postulate not very convincing. For example Khurana[18] observes thus:

> "Earnings after tax and lagged dividends are the primary determinants of dividend policy decision in all the industries under study... most of the companies treat lagged dividend and not lagged profit as a bench mark for making changes in the current year's dividend payment. Policy orientation of most companies is to treat dividend decision a `primary and active' decision variable in their financial policy making".

In a similar manner Rao & Sharma[19] find as follows:

> "In view of the financial stringencies impounded by the capital market the firms are constrained to depend on the internal finances and so as not to displease the existing shareholders, the firms consider the dividend decision as primary to reduce antagonism".

It may be stated that unlike the USA practice Indian companies are obligated not to issue bonus shares in lieu of cash dividends which would, perhaps, imply that the future dividend liability of the companies are likely to increase even if the current dividend is alteast maintained. In all such cases issuance of bonus shares may have an effect on current market prices based on anticipated improved dividend prospects and may then form part of a conscious current resource allocation strategy for several companies if not all.

Capital Market[20], a financial fortnightly published from Bombay, has tabulated data on bonus distribution of 150 Indian public limited listed companies. This effort makes a subjective classification of companies following certain benchmarks and accompanying variables even if explicit *ex-ante* bonus policies have not been existing. Examples are given of companies issuing bonus shares according to the following implicit patterns as given in Table -1.3.

Table - 1.3

Bonus Share Issues in India - Observed Patterns

Bench Mark	Accompanying Variable	No. of Companies
1. Target Book Value	-	18
2. Target EPS	-	3
3. Frequent & Liberal Bonus issues	Low or medium cash dividends	11
4. Small Bonus ratios	Large Cash dividends	2
5. Frequent & Large Bonus ratios	High cash dividends	20
6. Bonus at the earliest instant	-	11

Signaling Effect

Peter C. Eisemann and Edward A. Moses[21] surveyed the opinions of managers of both stock dividend paying and non-paying companies as to their motivations for issuing stock dividends. The survey results as reported clearly indicate that some managers feel that the shareholders do gain from stock dividend though many of them have read the finance literature and are aware of its generally negative conclusions. Also, majority of the respondents from both the groups felt that stock dividends ultimately increase the members of the firm. Managers of stock dividend paying companies overwhelmingly agreed that replacing cash dividends with stock dividend would increase sharehlders' after tax receipts since shareholders could sell the stock dividends and pay taxes on the gain at the capital gains tax rate, while they would have to pay taxes on cash dividends at the ordinary income tax rate. In regard to the second component of stockholders' return — the value of stock holding — while non- stock dividend paying group did not agree as strongly, both groups felt that stock prices would not fully adjust to occasional stock dividends. The stock dividend paying group strongly agreed that stock dividends enable management to express their confidence in the firm, suggesting that stock dividends might have some information content.

Tylor W.Foster III and Don Vikrey[22] have confirmed the feelings of managers about the stock dividends having some information content by testing the information content of stock dividend announcement. They examined the aggregate market reaction around the declaration dates of a sample of stock dividends that had no other concurrent announcement recorded in the Wall Street Journal so that the possible stock dividend effect was highlighted. In the first instant, they expected the unexpected returns to occur on the declaration date. Their second premise was that the sample stock dividends would tend to produce positive unexpected returns. Using 'z' statistic they tested the following hypotheses:

1. The mean of the unexpected returns of the population from which their declaration date sample was drawn is less than or equal to zero.

2. The mean of the unexpected returns of the population from which their ex-date sample was drawn is less than or equal to zero.

Their test result is presented in Table - 1.4.

Table - 1.4

Summary of Market Efficiency Related Tests

	Sample mean	Sample St. Dev.	Standard Error	'z' Values	Critical Values	Hypothesis Tested
Declaration date residuals	.0201	.0377	.00416	4.828	2.24	1
ex-date residuals	.0064	.395	.00436	1.467	2.24	2

It is clear that the mean of the unexpected returns of the population from which ex-date sample was drawn is less than or equal to zero. However, the mean of unexpected returns of the population from which declaration sample was drawn is not less than or equal to zero. Therefore, the ultimate implications of these findings appear to be that the market, in the aggregate, uses stock dividend information (or some consistent information) in setting equilibrium security price; that a significant portion of the reaction to this information occurs on its public release date; that such information tends to generate Positive Unexpected Returns; and that the market is not conditioned to react positively to stock dividends information on the ex-date. Here three things become evident: 1. declaration of stock dividend do have information content, 2. the market reacts to such information the moment it becomes public, 3. the market does not wait for its reaction until the ex-date because by that time the information with regard to stock dividend already becomes public and is impounded in the market pricing process.

Many shareholders regard stock dividends as distributions of corporate earnings equal to the fair value of the additional shares received by them. Such a view gets quite strengthened when the bonus ratio is a small proportion of equity shares outstanding. In an event like this, bonus shares will not have any apparent effect on the share price so that the market value of the previously held shares remains substantially unchanged. Such a phenomenon suggests market inefficiency because in perfect markets the expected price adjustment as on the ex-dividend date is: the last closing price prior to the ex-date divided by (1+Bonus ratio). J. Randall Woolridge[23] has tested the validity of this hypothesis through an investigation into the day prior closing to ex-date opening and ex-date closing price, and established that stock prices do not fully adjust for stock dividend and consequently, stock dividend increases the value of the stock holdings. This may be because of the market imperfections, market inefficiency or both. It is argued that indivisibility, taxes, and transaction costs are market imperfections at least partially responsible for abnormal ex-date returns. In other words, because of the presence of the market imperfections and market inefficiency the shareholder stands a chance to gain value for his holdings on ex-date of stock dividend.

Another study with a very interesting conclusion relating to the signaling effect and information content of stock dividend and stock split was by Mark S. Grinblatt, Ronald W. Masulis and Sheridan Titman[24]. They found not only that there is a valuation effect for a 'pure' split or stock dividend, but that this valuation change, for the most part, cannot be explained by forecasts of near term increases in cash dividends. In addition, the announcement effect is larger for the stock dividend sample than for the stock split sample. They have also established that, on an average, there is a significant increase in a firm's stock price at the announcement and that, in general, this upward revision of the firm's value cannot be attributed to any other contemporaneous announcements. They state that this increase may be partially due to forecasts of imminent increases in cash dividends, but a sub-sample of stocks that paid no dividends in the three years prior to the announcement displays similar price behaviour. Thus, they conclude, some of the information content of stock distributions appear to be directly associated with firm's future cash flows.

Before going to summarise the literature on the theme, we identified the empirically tested opinion into two broad schools of logic: 1. those who have found a positive relationship of stock dividends on (measuring the effect from the announcement date) stock prices or value of the firm; and 2. those who have not been able to uncover any such positive relationship. In very general terms the case of positive relationship had been found to exist in circumstances where stock dividend has been substantial, non-periodic or occasional and unexpected by an average investor. A vast chunk of these investigations has used the US corporate stock price data. However, such an evidence is not yet adequately available in the Indian Context.

Issue of bonus shares has almost gone unnoticed in India as an empirically testable proposition. The one study, already referred to, is by Gupta who presents copious statistical evidence to conclude[25]:

> "... an improvement in the valuation of an enterprise as a result of bonus issue can be maintained only if, and to the extent that, bonus issue is followed up by an increase in the quantum of dividend payment."

He further states that bonus shares do influence the share prices even though the effect is not consistently substantial over time and span. At one point Gupta even considers bonus shares analogous with stock splits of the US kind. While this may be true in a sense that stock splits in US are as nearly infrequent as in India. The basic difference between the two in effect might relate to the principal object being persecuted. Thus, the driving consideration of stock splits is to improve the marketability of shares by bringing them within a low price trading range whereas the one for stock dividends is to capitalise the growing accruals to the reserves account and incidentally to broaden both the ownership and market of the shares.

This review of empirical studies in the realm of stock dividends, stock splits and bonus shares highlighted a few important issues in the area. Following are the specific issues that were covered by various studies.

1. Is it possible for the investors to realise excess returns produced by the bonus shares specifically the capital gains and consequential tax effects thereof on or around the announcement date/or ex-date?

2. In the event of bonus issues producing excess returns, to what extent can these be attributed to bonus issue *quo* bonus issues? In other words, is it possible to delineate the excess returns effect of bonus issues from those of other fundamental factors.

Expectations of Managements and Investors

The most crucial aspect pertains to the first question which is concerned with the expectations of management and investors built upon announcement of bonus shares. Ross (1977) Leland and Pyle (1977) and Bhattacharya (1979) reported in their works that financial decisions convey information which affect the value of the firm. In testing their proposition they assumed that 1. information between management and investors is asymmetric, 2. managers have an incentive to convey favourable information to investors, and that 3. it is prohibitively costly for low value firms to mimic the finance decisions of high value firms. It must be stated that the traditional signaling hypothesis imposed a condition for the signaling effect to fructify that conveying information through financial decisions must involve a cost. As there are no apparent costs involved in the issue of bonus shares this should have no information content according to the traditional signaling view. However, a few arguments have been adduced in favour of signaling effect of bonus shares/stock dividends despite the non-presence of apparent costs associated with them by Grinblatt, Masulis, and Titman in their study[25].

The first argument has been recognised as 'retained earnings hypothesis'[26]. According to this, the value of the newly distributed shares is subtracted from retained earnings and added to the firm's capital account. If the firm faces legal restrictions or has bond covenants written in terms of retained earnings the additional shares can further restrict the firm's ability to pay cash dividends in future. Therefore, only those firms with higher expected future earnings will issue bonus shares and so that, the issue of bonus shares is a signal of expected prosperous future of the company. This view is further strengthened by the studies of Khurana who found that the dividend decision of the firm is an active policy variable for management and affects the value. He further analyses through his data that the effect of dividend on share prices accrues with a time lag of one accounting period which implies that the previous year's dividend provides a signaling effect for the coming years's dividend and share price.

It may also be postulated that there are indirect costs associated with false signaling such as loss of reputation. Firms usually, but not always, reveal their information truthfully. Communication of information through financial decisions like stock dividends would have some information content even if they are not perfect. This is referred to as the 'reputation model' or 'reputation hypothesis'[27].

It has also been found that stock dividends 'call attention' to the firm and market analysts begin reassessing the firm's future cash flows in their wake. It is obvious that such reassessment will find favour with under-priced firms but not with over-priced firms. Recognised in literature as the 'attention hypothesis', this view emphasises that the price effect on the announcement date reflects the average under pricing of the firm that elects to issue stock dividends. Since management reveals the value of the firm only partially there is adequate reason for subsequent reassessment being done by analysts. It must be noted that both the reputation and attention hypotheses do not explain why firms use financial decisions like stock dividends to convey information and do not issue press releases directly. May be firms do not want open public disclosure to restrict their position from competitors. It is also considered that they are averse to the risk of being proved wrong and exposing themselves for possible suits for damages by stock holders.

It may be that managers do not intend to convey information through a stock dividend. Conventional wisdom suggests that such financial decisions are aimed at bringing the shares within a popular trading range. In this connection it can be observed that managers may decide not to issue stock dividends even if price of the firm's stock is high because they have some unfavourable inside information and they expect that future events will force the price of the share to fall below the popular trading range. This position can thus be utilised by investors to draw their inferences based on the fact that a stock dividend announcement and subsequent stock performance are correlated phenomenon. This is named as 'trading range hypothesis'[28]. A lacunae in this reasoning centers around some over-valued firms who may not be worried about the trading range of their stock and may announce a bonus issue just to obtain a temporary rise in its price, for example for raising fresh capital from market etc.

Although the foregoing hypotheses have not been formally developed as quantitative models, the results that followed are consistent with many of their implications and hence, the view that the stock dividends and similar other financial decisions are pure cosmetic events stands substantially rebutted.

V. Hypothesis

It will be seen that issue of bonus shares has got many interesting accounting, legal, and market implications. Our research literature also suggests that it might affect investors' and managers' expectations as also analysts' assessments and re-assessment through a signaling effect. The most vital question is whether bonus shares have or do not have immediate or lagged market value implications. We have cited numerous works relating to them and related aspects of bonus issues in broad context of financial decisions in the market oriented world.

We have also noticed that there has been a near absence of empirical research for the Indian Corporate Sector in this area. A series of research endeavours could therefore be addressed to this phenomenon. General observations based on press comments and random investor interaction do recommend that bonus shares are keenly awaited and widely guessed for their price effects both by the fundamentalists and technical analysts. Investors in general regard bonus announcement as a favourable event of the market. All this encourages research in the first instance to be centered on the crucial question relating to the real tangible value of bonus shares for the owners of the firm. Without going into many complications being incorporated in our effort we have focused our attention on the following specific hypothesis:

> "Bonus shares unless followed by an increase in the cash quantum of dividend will not generally increase the value of shares in the market. The usual phenomenon of market price run-up in anticipation of or in the wake of rumours about bonus issues is primarily caused by higher dividend pay-out (not necessarily ratio) expectations of the market."

The study is premised on the following assumptions:

1. Market valuation process is rational in the sense that the market participants are active and they prefer *inter alia,* bigger gains to smaller gains and early gains to later gains.
2. The period of study is not characterised by long spells of thin trading activity and bonus holidaying moods of companies.
3. The companies follow, honour and do not attempt directly or indirectly to by-pass the guidelines for bonus issues made under the Companies Act, and Control of Capital Issues Act.

VI. Methodology

This section provides a very broad and brief description of sources of information, nature and extent of information used, the size and selection of sample, and techniques of analysis for processing and interpreting data.

Information relating to bonus issues by companies has been compiled from the Bombay Stock Exchange Directory updated upto June 1989. We considered the financial year in which bonus shares are actually allotted and transfer of funds from the reserves to the paid-up capital account took place as the year of bonus issue. Where ever the financial year is at a deviation from 12 months period the data related to that year is considered on annualised basis so as to bring in comparability in the analysis. The data that is so compiled has been compared with the other sources of information like the annual reports of the companies, Kothari Industrial Guide, Directory of Indian Companies on a random basis and the accuracy verified. We could thus gather information of 259 companies with 435 bonus issues. This data is used to analyse the characteristic features and post-bonus dividend tracts of the Indian Corporate Sector. While the focus under characteristic features of the bonus issues is on identifying the number and frequency of bonus issues, popular bonus ratios, trends in the amounts being capitalised, the size of the bonus issuing companies and on the extent of capitalisation of reserves during the study period, the section on post-bonus dividend tracts is specifically addressed to analyse the size, quantum and rates of cash dividend in the bonus years and during subsequent years to reckon the post-bonus corporate payout behaviour and the dividend advantage/disadvantage[29] to shareholders.

So as to ascertain the fundamental data pertaining to different phases of bonus issue, an 'Information Schedule' was prepared and sent to 295 companies who are said to have issued bonus shares at least once during 1977 and 1988 and with a reminder we could have responses from 69 companies covering 119 bonus issues. The BSE has kindly permitted us to gather 'announcement dates' for another 77 bonus issues made between 1977-88 by companies whose shares are categorised under the list of specified shares from its official files. Thus in all we have information relating to the announcement date for 196 bonus issues. This information is used for the purpose of analysing the bonus effect on price.

Since on the recommendation of the 'Board' a resolution approving the proposed capitalisation should be passed by the shareholders of the company before an application is made to the CCI, it is originally the 'Board' that takes a decision in the form of recommendation to the shareholders with respect to the issue of bonus shares. As per the listing agreement the company is bound to inform the stock exchange about the date on which the Board is meeting to consider the bonus proposal. Consequently, the news of bonus becomes public the moment stock exchange receives an official communication from the company about the date of Board meeting where bonus proposal will be considered. Therefore, the date on the which the stock exchange receives the official communication about the proposed Board Meeting where the bonus proposal shall be considered is for all practical purposes the 'announcement date'. We are aware of the fact that there are a few cases of bonus being turned down either in the Board Meeting or by the CCI at a later date. Since our sample contains only those announcements that have materialised, our definition of announcement date will not lead to any interpretational ambiguity. In fact, the average time lag between the day of informing the stock exchange and the Board Meeting day is not over a week for most of the issues included in this study.

In order to measure the bonus impact on the price we considered the 'base date' to be 90 days before the announcement date. This will provide a provision to eliminate the possible pre-announcement leakage consequences on the price. For the risk of leakage is likely to cause disastrous price swings in a volatile market, the companies about to decide in favour of bonus, when capital market conditions are highly uncertain, make it a point to minimise the advance time before formal announcement. Now that the Board Meetings are mostly held every month for most of the companies, managements will be presumed to take a rational decision of minimising the period between 'formative idea' of bonus and 'formal announcement'. Given explicit guidelines and managements' discretion the market anticipation is on surer grounds and though there is a risk of leakage the consequences are not expected to be that severe. External guessing may have a longer time gap but this time gap between external guessing and internal forming up has little relevance. The longer the time gap weaker the influence. Thus, from managements' point of view the leakage period is minimised as it is desirable and therefore six settlement periods before announcement date would ideally provide for the possible leakage.

The other dates of price comparison are as follows:

1. 30 days before announcement date.
2. 15 days before announcement date.
3. Announcement date.
4. 15 days after announcement date.
5. 30 days after announcement date.
6. 90 days after announcement date.
7. 180 days after announcement date.
8. 270 days after announcement date.
9. 365 days after announcement date.

We have not considered the period beyond a year after the announcement date because of the difficulty in tracing and isolating the implications of multifarious factors on the share price.

The closing price quotations as on different dates mentioned above of various bonus issuing companies have been compiled from the Daily Official List of the BSE. If the price on any specified date is not available either because that day being a non-trading day for the stock exchange or because the security was not traded on that day, the price quotation available immediately preceding that day has been taken. The ex-bonus prices have been adjusted according to the bonus ratio[30] to make the ex-bonus prices comparable to cum-bonus prices. There are around 25 companies whose shares have been either consolidated (reverse split) or split during the study period. The post-event (split or reverse split) prices of such shares are also adjusted in consonance with the ratio of such an event. Three of the sample bonus issues are either followed or accompanied with splits. Though aware of the split specific price implications we have not excluded these bonus issues from the sample since it has been thought the weightage of such events is negligible on aggregate result.

The post-bonus price changes need not necessarily be a result of bonus issue. The prominent among the other factors acting upon the price is the general market movement. The degree of association between security price and market is a function of multitudinous factors and in fact is very difficult to measure and isolate the general market implications on a security price. We attempted to isolate this by adjusting the price relatives at different points of time to the BSE Sensitive Index [BSESI] converted to the respective new bases, i.e., the price of security and the BSESI on base date equal to 100.

As mentioned earlier, a possible price contamination by a concurrent dividend announcement has been avoided by including only 'pure bonus announcements' in the sense that they are not associated with any other announcement relating to the dividends. This has been ensured on the basis of the response given by the companies to the last question in the 'Information Schedule' and by verifying the company communication to the stock exchange about the bonus issue from the files maintained by the stock exchange.

VII. Plan of the Study

The present chapter formulated the problem and hypothesis with a statement of objectives, scope of the study, a review of literature, an outline of the assumptions and the research methodology.

The following chapter provides an overview of the theoretical and legal underpinnings related to the issue of bonus shares.

Third chapter discusses the characteristic features of bonus issues made in India during 1977-88. This is an empirical retrospect of bonus issues in India.

Fourth chapter deals with an analysis of the post- bonus dividend tracks followed by companies. Specifically, the size, quantum and rates of cash dividends in the bonus years and during subsequent years have been analysed with a view to reckon the corporate pay-out behaviour.

Fifth chapter specifically explores the nature and degree of relationship between bonus issue and share prices.

Sixth chapter contains a summary of the major findings and conclusions.

Notes and References

1. For a dividend announcement effect, see Petti (1972), Ahamy & Swary (1980), Kwan (1981), Eades (1982), Asquith & Mullins (1983) and Brickley (1983). For capital structure changes see Masulis (1980a, 1980b, 1983), Dan (1981) and Vermaelen (1981)
2. Lintner: "Distributions of Incomes of Corporations Among Dividends, Retained Earnings, and Taxes", American Economic Review, XLVI, (May, 1956), pp. 97-113.
3. Michaelsen: "The Determinants of Dividend Policies: A Theoretical and Empirical Study", University of Chicago, 1961.
4. Undiluted dividend distribution is a situation where a) when the dividend rate is maintained in tact; b) when the dividend rate is increased; and c) when the dividend rate is less proportionately lowered when compared to the bonus ratio.
5. Features of Major Stock Exchanges in India as on 31.3.1989

	Listed Stocks		Listed Companies		Brokers		Turnover	
	No.	%	No.	%	No.	%	Rs. in crores	%
Bombay	4767	35.32	2275	30.20	533	29.96	20563	48.66
Calcutta	3942	29.20	2254	29.91	659	37.04	12942	30.63
Delhi	2830	20.96	1789	23.74	122	6.86	2044	4.84
Ahme'bad	1008	7.47	661	8.77	299	16.81	1368	3.24
Madras	952	7.05	556	7.38	166	9.33	5338	12.63
Total	13499	100.00	7535	100.00	1779	100.00	42255	100.00

Source: Compiled from Tables - 2.5, 4.4, and 4.5 of a study on "The State of Capital Market 1988-89" by The Securities and Exchanges Board of India. pp. S5, S31-32.

6. The size criteria being a) paid-up capital of Rs. 10 lakhs or more but below Rs. 50 lakhs for medium size and b) paid-up capital of Rs. 50 lakhs or above for large size.
7. Some of the examples of cases excluded on this basis are: issues made to erstwhile holders of deferred shares as a part of scheme of conversion into equity shares; issues made to financial institutions in exercise of the convertibility clauses in loan agreements; or issues made without payment in executing the contract.
8. The hurdle dates governing the inclusion criteria for the period have been stated in the scope of the study.
9. It may be noted that the country had passed through a number of politico-economic instabilities during 1970's like Bangladesh War (December, 1971), advent of Jai Prakash Narain's Total Revolution (1973-74), imposition of emergency (1975-76), emergence of Janata Government, the nationalisation of Indian Copper Industry, take over of Indian Iron and Steel (1972), the anti-inflationary package including the Dividend Restriction Ordinance, 1974, an upward revision of Bank Rate twice during 1970s and a continuous stock market recession beginning in 1974 are some of such examples of extraordinary events.
10. C.Austin Barker: "Evaluation of Stock Dividends", Harvard Business Review, Vol. XXXVI, July-August, 1958, pp. 99-114.
11. USA practice of issuing stock dividends is not analogous to Indian practice of issuing bonus

shares. The former has a regular periodicity and dividend rate and usually low (for further analytical clarifications see chapter - II supra.)

12. Cohen and Zinberg: Investment Analysis and Portfolio Management, (Irwin) 1967
13. Van Horne: Financial Management and policy, (Prentice Hall), 1968.
14. Gupta. L.C., Bonus Shares, Macmillan India, 1973.
15. Ibid, pp. 28. For further theoretical explanations of this part see chapter - II supra.
16. Gupta. L.C., Bonus Shares: Facts, Fiction and Policy: Chartered Accountant, Vol. XXVII, No.2, Aug. 1978.
17. F. Modigliani and M.H. Miller: "The Cost of Capital, Corporation Finance and the Theory of Investment", American Economic Review, Vol. 148 (June 58) pp. 261-77.
18. P.K. Khurana: "Corporate Dividend Policy in India", Panchsheel Pub., New Delhi, pp. 99.
19. T.V.S. Rammohan Rao & Rita Sharma: "Primacy of Corporate Dividend Decisions", Indian Economic Journal Vol.32, No.2, pp. 56-72.
20. Capital Market: Special Number on Distribution Index, April, 1989, pp. 14-22.
21. Peter C.Eisemann and Edward A. Moses: "Stock Dividends: Managements' View", Financial Analysts Journal, July/August, 1978, pp. 77-80.
22. Tylor W. Foster III and Don Vikrey: "The Information Content of Stock Dividend Announcement", The Accounting Review, Vol. LIII, No.2, April, 1978.
23. J. Randall Woolridge: "Ex-date Stock Price Adjustment to Stock Dividend: A Note", Journal of Finance, Vol. XXXVII, March, 1983, pp. 247-255.
24. Mark S.Grinblatt, Ronald W. Masulis and Sheridan Titmann: "The Valuation Effects of Stock Splits and Stock Dividend", Journal of Financial Economics, Vol. 13 (1984), pp. 461-490.
25. Ibid. pp. 107.
26. a. Henn, H., 1970, "Hand Book of the Law of Corporations and other Business Enterprises", West Publishing Co., St. Paul, pp. 650-672.

    b. Simmons, Richard, 1972, "Drafting of Commercial Bank Loan Agreements", Business Lawyer, 28, pp. 196.
27. Heinkel.R., 1984, "A Theory of Credibility: Cost Less Signals in a Rational Expectations, Infinite Horizon Model", Working Paper (University of British Columbia, Vancouver).
28. Akerlof.G., 1970, "The Market for `lemons': Quality Uncertainity and the Market Mechanism", Quarterly Journal of Economics, 84, pp. 448-500.
29. The dividend advantage/disadvantage is the relative change in the bonus adjusted post-bonus dividend rate to the pre-bonus dividend rate.

    $$\text{Magnitude of dividend change} : \frac{[\{D_b \times (1+b)\} - D_a]}{D_a} \times 100$$

    Where D_b = Post-bonus dividend rate

    b = Bonus rate

    D_a = Pre-bonus dividend rate
30. Cum-bonus price is [1+b] times the ex-bonus price where 'b' is the bonus ratio.

II

Bonus Shares — Theoretical and Legal Underpinnings

I. Introduction

The purpose of this chapter is to offer a clarification with regard to certain important concepts used in this empirical research investigation addressed to the problem of uncovering a relationship between bonus shares and value of the firm. Most of these terms and concepts have finance, accounting and legal orientations. The attempt includes the term 'bonus shares' itself and extends to distinguishing the 'bonus shares' from 'rights shares'. There are a few terms which appear similar in meaning and characteristics to bonus shares, but, nevertheless, have certain distinctive features. This chapter makes an effort to underline such features also. The second part of the chapter summarises and explains legal aspects of bonus shares in India analysing the appropriate official guidelines issued from time to time and also relevant tax provisions.

Part-A of the chapter opens up with a description of the nature of bonus shares and their accounting implications. It is followed by an explanation of what stock dividends are. This part then provides an over-view of sub-divided shares and attempts a distinction between stock splits and bonus shares. Part-A concludes with a clarification on the nature of Rights Shares and their salient features which distinguish them from bonus shares. Part-B of the chapter summarises the legal environment for the sanction and issue of bonus shares and provides an update on official guidelines governing the issuance of bonus shares. It also includes an analysis of tax provisions and implications related to bonus shares.

Part-A: Conceptual Analysis

II. Bonus Shares

Bonus shares are seen by most investors as 'gift' from the issuing companies. Even though the legal definition of the term does not center around the gift concept, popular market reaction to bonus issues revolves around it. Bonus shares are expected by the investors and the market 'over and above' the usual cash dividends. The implications of bonus issues in this sense would be that it will appear as a variable in the valuation equation of the firm because the shareholders put an additional worth on it even if there is no direct consideration flowing from them.

That the gift flows from the company to shareholder has *raisen d' atre* the 'Board' of the company have the powers to deploy the resources including the ones created out of internal accumulations. The legal position is that the shareholders cannot claim dividends as a matter of right except when the 'Board' fraudulently attempts to deny the distribution[1]. There is one more circumstance in which the 'Board' will not have absolute freedom in appropriating current profits for reserves. This will be so when a transfer of reserves exceeds 10 percent of current profits after tax is contemplated. In such situations 1) if the companies transfer voluntarily a higher percentage of profits to reserves (i.e., when it exceeds 10% of net profits after tax) the dividends declared by the companies shall be the average rate of dividend declared in the three years immediately preceding the financial year and 2) if the company has issued bonus shares in the financial year in which dividend is declared or in the three financial years immediately preceding the financial year, the dividend declared in the three years immediately preceding the financial year. Minimum distribution of dividend in the above two cases need not be ensured if the net profits after tax in the current year is lower by 20% or more than the average net profits after tax of the two financial years immediately preceding the current financial year. At the same time managements are under an obligation to retain a part of the profits as per the requirements of the Companies Act, 1956.[2] Research on dividends and dividend policies clearly indicates that retention at a time when the company needs funds for growth will not be protested against by the shareholders[3]. It will be seen that reserves accumulate partly in compliance with the legal requirements and partly as a result of the 'Board' discretion. And when these accumulations assume a particular size the directors are pleased to share this additional prosperity of the company with investors. The decision to issue bonus shares generally comes in this form and is subject to the official guidelines with regard to the quantum of issues. That the bonus shares are a gesture of good will and a token of gift from the 'Board' to shareholders is thus clearly seen from the foregoing analysis. It may be added, however, that this gift is not personal but has corporate institutional foundations.

Even though bonus shares are ostensibly regarded by shareholders as something of real value the theoretical position is that they are created and effectuated by an accounting transfer from free reserves to the paid up capital account. The consequence is that the liabilities side of the Balance Sheet which is the origin for bonus shares accounting remains unaffected in the aggregate by the issuance of such shares. There is, of course, a quantitative change between the two major components of the net worth viz., Paid Up Capital which increases and Free Reserves which decrease. It will thus be seen that the issuance of bonus shares brings about a change in the components of net worth but keeps total net worth unaltered. In other words, the aggregate equity of the shareholder in the company remains constant in spite of bonus issues.

The company issuing these shares in a certain stipulated ratio has to be in conformity with the guidelines and is always subject to sanction by appropriate authorisations. The fact of the matter is that the number of shares outstanding on the capital structure of a company increases in the wake of bonus issues. This is the other change on the capital components of a Balance sheet of a company apart from the change in the components of net worth as noted above. The combined effect of these two changes is that per share Net-Worth declines. The extent to which Net worth per share or Book Value Per share (BVPS) declines is shown below:

Let
V = Pre-Bonus BVPS
B = Bonus Rate
Then post bonus BVPS = (V/(1+B))
Decline in BVPS = (V - (V/(1+B))
or V [1 - {1/(1+B)}] or V (B/(1+B))

Thus it is clear that the Net Worth per share is reduced by (B/(1+B)) percent.

To illustrate numerically:

Let the pre-bonus Net Worth Structure be assumed as follows: Paid-up capital: 10 lakh shares @ Rs. 10/- = Rs. 100 lakhs

Free Reserves:	= Rs. 100 lakhs
Net Worth	= Rs. 200 Lakhs

BVPS = (Rs. 200 Lakhs/10 Lakh) = Rs. 20/-

Assuming a bonus issue in the ratio of 1:2 the post bonus Net Worth Structure will be as under:

Paid-up capital : 15 Lakh shares @ Rs. 10/-	= Rs. 150 Lakhs
Free Reserves:	= Rs. 50 Lakhs
Net Worth	= Rs. 200 Lakhs

Post bonus BVPS = (Rs. 200 lakhs/15 lakhs) = Rs. 13.33/-
Decline in BVPS = (Rs. 20 - Rs. 13.33) = Rs. 6.67/-

Using the formula derived above

V = Rs. 20
B = 0.50
Decline in BVPS = Rs. 20(1-(1/1+.5))) = Rs. 6.67/-
The Rate of Decline = (B/(1+B)) = (.5/(1+.5)) = 0.33
or 33% or (6.67/20) x 100 = 33%

Per share Net Worth after bonus will remain unchanged only if the total Net Worth increases at any future date (either in the wake of fresh issue or as a result of a larger appropriation of operating surplus to free reserves) in the same proportion as the bonus rate. An important point to bear in mind is that inter temporal comparisons of the per share accounting and financial variables will be vitiated and will need correction for the diminution or dilution that is brought by additional number of shares in the wake of a bonus decision. The observations with regard to diminution and dilution of per share net worth applies equally to other per share accounting and financial variable like Earning Per Share, Dividend Per Share, Book Value Per Share, Market Capitalisation Per share etc.

Bonus shares will generally have same Par or Nominal Value as existing equity shares of the company. Also they are given in the same type of shares as already owned by shareholders. If any other type of share is given it is technically considered as a property dividend and therefore, fully and immediately taxable as income under the US Law. This practice, however, does not prevail in India.

Issue of bonus shares has no immediate effect upon assets as there is no net increase in funds with which to acquire new assets. However, there are important market implications of bonus shares. Though an individual shareholder has a large number of shares after a bonus issue, his equity stake in the business has not changed in amount. It is simply represented now by a larger number of transferable capital units. All this is not to suggest that nothing happens in the wake of a bonus and that this is at best a non-event. In fact, market never ignores a bonus issue and prices do fluctuate in accordance with investor expectations about the net enlargement of their flows in the form of future dividends. Such flows are capitalised by the investors and prices correspondingly move up. The opposite would happen if the size of the dividends is less than market expectations because investors would now capitalise a reduced expected future flow. It may be noted that this consequence follows with the capitalisation rate remaining constant.

III. Stock Dividends

Capitalisation of reserves and issuing of additional shares is not a unique practice of the Indian corporate sector alone. In the USA this is known as 'stock dividends. Distributions made in the form of stock are of three kinds: viz., 'extraordinary', 'periodic' and 'substitutional'[4]. An extraordinary stock dividend is one that capitalises a substantial part of the accumulated surplus of past years and gives the shareholders additional shares. The periodic stock dividends are those that capitalise part of the current year's earnings only. A substitutional stock dividend is declared in place of the cash dividend.

Extra dividends of spectacular type being large in amount and infrequent in occurrence are called as 'melon'.[5] Melon cuttings and rumours of them are great incentives for speculators. There is sometimes a long series of rumours preceding a melon cutting. At other times the transaction is announced suddenly and catches many unawares. It can serve useful purpose either way. As a matter of fact, melon cutting is so often tinged with suspicion that its appearance always causes one to question who is securing an advantage from its use.

The Indian scenario with respect to the issue of bonus appears to be analogous with melon cuttings. The bonus share episodes of ACC in 1984 and Bombay Dyeing in 1988 are examples.

ACC was the largest cement manufacturer in the country accounting for about 31.4 percent of the installed capacity, 31.7 percent of production and 31.8 percent of sales in 1983 with 17 production units well dispersed all through the country employing 30,000 people and about 62,000 shareholders who are widely distributed. Among the top companies in the private sector in 1982-83, ACC ranked third in terms of total assets and seventh in terms of sales. ACC was eligible for issuing bonus shares during 1984 in terms of the then existing guidelines. ACC satisfied the time lag test as the previous bonus issue was made in June 1980. The residual reserves test would permit the company to capitalise about Rs. 61 crores and the yield test would have allowed it to capitalise around Rs. 44 crore. However the maximum amount that could be capitalised would be limited to Rs. 33.23 crores which happened to be its paid up capital then. ACC earned an after tax profit of Rs. 21.20 crores in 1983-84 as against Rs. 32.20 crores in 1982-83. The management is understood to have been affirmed that the company would be able to maintain a dividend of 20 percent on the expanded capital resulting from a bonus of 3:5 at least for the next two years. Thus in all accounts it appeared the company to be fully eligible to make a bonus in the ratio not less than 2:5. During the last week of September, 1984 the company sent a notice to the Bombay Stock Exchange (BSE) stating that the Board of Directors of the company would meet on October 22, 1984 for finalising the accounts for the year ending July 31, 1984, for recommending the dividend for the year and for considering an issue of bonus shares. On October 22, 1984 the Board took a decision to drop the much awaited and talked about bonus issue at the instance of the financial institutions.

The share once considered to be widow's share shot up to an unprecedented high and appeared to be the most sought after scrip by speculators on the stock market. The immediate provocation seems to be a statement made by the Chairman in the Annual General Meeting during December, 1983 that the company would make a bonus issue as early as possible and when it is in the interest of the shareholders. From a low of Rs.299 on May 26, 1984 the share price climbed to a high of Rs.460 on October 12, 1984. The information about the financial institutions opposing the ACC bonus presumably leaked on October 20, 1984, just 48 hours prior to the Board meeting of ACC. Investors and speculators had not taken such a beating in one scrip as they did in the ACC share just prior to Diwali. There was a perpendicular fall in the share value from Rs.460 to Rs.355 in the course of just two days of trading, the first in kerb and the second at a special session held on *Dhan Teras* day on October 22 by the BSE ignoring its 50 year old tradition of not trading on pre Diwali day. Losses to investors and speculators are placed at around Rs.3 to Rs.4 crores. The BSE authorities, fearing a crisis on the stock exchange prohibited fresh sales of ACC scrips. The brokers were permitted only to squaring up their out standing business; also purchases which could be carried over from one settlement to another were allowed. On the other hand fresh sales could be effected only if the share certificates were in their possession and delivery was to have made at the end of settlement.[6]

Another similar case was of Bombay Dyeing. On July 14, 1988 the price of the company among the pivotals moved rather in a relatively wide range on alternate bouts of buying and selling on the eve of the company's Board meeting. Despite a very encouraging reported performance the shares led the down-trend dropping sharply on heavy bull liquidation because of the rejection of bonus issue by the Board on July 14, 1988. It slumped sharply by Rs.7.50 to Rs.111.50 on bear hammering. On July 15th it further declined from Rs.11 to close at Rs.102.50 on selling of over 30,000 shares with a net loss of 17 points.[7]

Events of this nature will lead one to conclude that the share market looks upon the policy of issuing bonus shares with 'mythical reverence' not substantiated by the facts and events as they shape up around the declaration of bonus issues. In other words there appears to be a powerful pull of guess estimates and even rumours.[8]

IV. Subdivided Shares

Section 94 (1) (b) and (c) of the Companies Act, 1956 permits a company having a share capital and in pursuance of the power conferred by the articles, and in General Meeting, to consolidate and divide all or any of its shares into shares of larger and lessor amount than the existing shares or convert all or any of the paid up shares into stock and reconvert stock into paid up shares of any denomination. The par value is reduced through subdivision and as a result the number of shares outstanding increases. Shares of reduced par value are known as subdivided shares.

Unlike bonus shares, the subdivision of shares will not affect the amount in reserves account. This subdivision of shares, by its very nature, is similar to the stock split of the USA. A discussion on stock split is taken up in the section that follows.

V. Stock Split

Subdividing the outstanding stock units, without changing the paid up capital is known as stock split. Through stock split the par value of the stock is reduced and the number of shares outstanding, naturally, gets multiplied.

Stock dividends and splits appear to be similar to each other although they are typically used for different purposes. It must be observed that stock dividends are announced over and above the cash dividends except in an unusual circumstance when they are of substitutional in nature. As noted later stock splits are employed to reduce the market price of a share. From an accounting point there is a significant difference. In the USA accounting principles treat the value of the stock dividend as a transfer from retained earnings only for stock distributions of 20% or less. All stock distributions exceeding 25% are treated as splits and do not affect retained earnings. For stock distributions between 20-25% the accounting principles provide for corporte discretion, but are usually treated as stock dividends. Similar clarificatory guidelines are imposed by the American Institute of Certified Public Accountants (AICPA), Securities and Exchanges Commission (SEC), New York Stock Exchange (NYSE), and American Stock Exchange (AMEX) for stock distributions in the range of 20-25%. In other words, accounting principles treat a stock distribution in excess of 25% of the shares outstanding as a stock split whereas distributions less than 20 percent are classified as stock dividends.[9]

However, in India accounting principles do make a clear distinction between bonus shares and subdivision of shares. Irrespective of the percentage of distribution, issuance of bonus shares has to be done through a transfer of such amount from free reserves to the paid up capital. No such transfer is needed for subdivision.

A stock split or subdivision of share is usually reserved for occasions when a company wishes to achieve a substantial reduction in the market price per share and place the share in a more popular trading range, thereby attracting more buyers, provided that the results of the subdivision does not place the share in the 'cats and dogs' class. Experience demonstrates that lower stock prices but within the trading range increase the number of stockholders. Other purposes of subdivision are to conceal the distribution of large profits by reducing the rate per share; to facilitate the future sale of new capital issuings; to provide a basis for the exchange of shares in a merger plan; to please shareholders who expect such action as indicative of financial success; to permit listing of share.[10]

Most of the purposes outlined in the above section are relevant for stock dividends or bonus shares too. In fact stock dividends and stock splits are different from each other on account of the dominant purpose for which each is employed. Thus, stock split is associated with market price consequences and stock dividend is an accompaniment of cash dividend or sweetener to the equity investors.

VI. Rights

When a company issues additional equity capital the shares are offered to the existing shareholders on a *prorate* basis so as to give them an opportunity to maintain their proportional share in the total capital. Such shares offered to the existing shareholders as a matter of right are known as 'rights'. In other words, the privilege of subscribing to new issue of shares offered by a company to its shareholders is called rights. Rights are issued to shareholders in the form of negotiable warrants which must be exercised on or before expiration of a specified date.

Section 81 of the Companies Act, 1956 provides that where at any time after the expiration of two years from the date of incorporation of the company or after one year from the date of the first allotment of shares, which ever is earlier, a public company limited by shares, issues further shares within the limits of authorised capital, its directors must first offer such further shares to the existing holders of equity shares in proportion to the paid up value on their shares at the time of further issue.

When a special resolution has been made in the AGM about not offering rights, the company need not offer rights. Even an ordinary resolution of not offering rights duly approved by the Central Government will exempt the company from offering rights.

Subscribing to the rights is purely optional and the Companies Act stipulates that the shareholder must be given at least 15 days to decide his option. Unless the Articles provide otherwise the shareholder will have the right to renounce the offer of rights, either wholly or partially, in favour of some other person. The directors have the option to dispose the shares as they think fit if the rights are declined by the shareholder to whom the offer is made or if the person in whose favour the renunciation is made declines to buy the shares.

Table 2.1 summarises the discussion on bonus shares, subdivided shares and rights shares with a view to bring out their distinguishing features.

Table - 2.1

The Nature of Bonus Shares, Sub-Divided Shares & Rights

	Bonus Shares	Subdivided Shares	Rights
1. Do they increase the number of outstanding shares?	Yes	Yes	Yes
2. Will there be any change in the book value of a share?	Yes	Yes	Yes
3. Is there any change in the shareholders' aggreagate proportional ownership as measured by Net Worth as a percent of Total Assets?	No	No	Yes
4. Is there any cash flow between the shareholder and company?	No	No	Yes
5. Will there be any change in the paid up capital?	Yes	No	Yes
6. Will there be any change in Net Worth?	No	No	Yes
7. Will there be any change in shareholders' reserves?	Yes	No	No
8. Will there be any change in par Value of the Share?	No	Yes	No

Part-B: Legal Environment

VII. Law Relating to Sanction of Bonus Shares

The issue of bonus shares has a basic legal sanction in sec 205(3) [including the proviso of the Indian Companies Act, 1956]. This is a permissive clause and leaves a number of accounting and procedural details uncovered. Even the rules framed under the Act do not provide a coverage for the procedures governing the issue of such shares. Moreover, the bonus shares are issued by companies in a highly dynamic setting of performance including operational and profit performance. It has, therefore, been thought advisable that a set of consistent guidelines be issued from time to time incorporating and reflecting the environmental changes affecting, *inter alia*, the determination of the quantum of bonus, conditions of eligibility, maximum permissible bonus, pre-conditions for issue, time lags and leads required in initiating and consummating the issue process etc. The governing rationale behind the guidelines has always been the protection of shareholders' interest and also to restrain the company from incurring unmanageable future obligations with respect to dividends and subsequent bonuses. Guidelines make effort to preserve the reserves cushion intact so that funds needed for subsequent expansion and modernisation of manufacturing facilities may not suffer an undue impairment.

Under the Capital Issues Control Act, 1947 the issue of bonus shares requires the sanction of the Controller of Capital Issues [CCI]. Companies Act, 1956 has laid down certain stipulations regarding the procedure of bonus issues in section 96 (1). This section reads as follows:

Section 96(1): "The company in General Meeting may upon the recommendation of the Board resolve-

(a) that is desirable to capitalise any part of the amount for the time being standing to the credit of any of the company's reserve accounts, or to the credit of the profit and loss account, or otherwise available for distribution; and

(b) that such sum be accordingly set free for distribution in the manner specified in clause (a) amongst the members who would have been entitled thereto, if distributed by way of dividend and in the same proportion.

Thus, any company to issue bonus shares must get them recommended by the 'Board' and also duly ratified by the shareholders in the 'Annual General Meeting' [AGM]. In addition, the resolution should also speak of the treatment of "fractional certificates".

a company has two options in respect of fractional certificates:

i. It may forward the fractional certificates along with the share scrips to the shareholders with instructions to consolidate fractional certificates before a particular date or within any extended date. Thereafter, the holder of the fractional certificates lose their right to consolidate and the directors in accordance with the right conferred in the general resolution, consolidate the remaining fractional certificates and dispose off the shares in the market. The value realized in such a transaction should be paid to the holders of unconsolidated fractional certificates proportionately.

ii. Another method rather easy one, is not to forward the fractional certificates to shareholders. Instead the members' resolution authorises the directors to consolidate fractional certificates into shares and dispose off in the share market. The proceeds are proportionately distributed to the shareholders entitled to such fractional certificates.

Many companies in recent times, follow the second method which is considered to be administratively convenient.

The approval by the members is followed by application to the CCI in the prescribed form accompanied by relevant enclosures such as 'Board' resolution; General Meeting resolution; memorandum of association; Balance Sheets for the last three years; auditors' certificate; treasury challan; and industrial license copies etc.

Applications for such approvals were decided by the CCI on the basis of certain provisions related to the determination of business income until March, 1974. A few of such provisions are Section 205, Section 78, Section 80 and Section 96(2). They primarily deal with specifying the conditions for capitalisation of reserves, the reserves that can be capitalised and the method of capitalisation of reserves etc. These sections read as follows:

> Section 205[3]: "No dividend shall be payable except in cash provided that nothing in this subsection shall be deemed to prohibit the capitalisation of profits or reserves of a company for the purpose of issuing fully paid up bonus shares or paying up any amount for the time being unpaid on any shares held by the members of the company".
>
> Section 78(2) (a): "the share premium may be applied in paying up unissued shares of the company to be issued to members of the company as fully paid bonus shares."
>
> Section 80(5): "The capital redemption reserve may be applied by the company in paying up unissued shares of company to be issued to members of the company as fully paid up bonus shares."
>
> Section 96 (2): The sum aforesaid shall not be paid in cash but shall be applied, subject to the provisions contained in clause (3), either in or towards-
>
> (i) paying up any amounts for the time being unpaid on any shares held by such members respectively;
>
> (ii) paying up in full, unissued shares of the company to be allotted and distributed, credited as fully paid up, to and amongst such members in proportions aforesaid; or
>
> (iii) partly in the way specified in sub clause (i) and partly in that specified in sub clause (ii).

Bonus Guidelines - Historical Retrospect

In view of the very general and piecemeal treatment of the subject, the ambiguity continued to persist in the matter of approval of issue of bonus shares by CCI till for the first time in March 1974 specific bonus guidelines were issued by the Governmet. These guidelines have undergone a metamorphosis. Under the detailed guidelines issued in March 1974 companies were not allowed to issue bonus shares till the partly paid up shares, if any, were fully paid up. For the purpose of arriving at the reserves eligible for capitalisation, only genuine profits transferred to reserves, share premium collected in cash and development rebate reserve formed the major components. This is an extension of Section 78(2) and Section 80(5) of the Companies Act, 1956. Further the residual reserves after the proposed capitalisation were not to be less than 33.33 per cent of the increased capital after the issue of bonus shares. No bonus shares were permitted in lieu of dividend; no more than two bonus issues were allowed to a company within a time lag of at least 18 months. Another criterion which related to the post bonus earnings power of the company stated that 30% of the average profits before tax should yield a rate of return on the expanded capital base of the company at 9%.

This attempt of the Central Government in bringing out a set of clearly spelled out guidelines on bonus was a pioneering move in creating a concrete and verifiable base for the CCI to scrutinise and regulate the issue of bonus shares by the private corporate sector and would dispel the uncertainty, to certain extent, that used to surround the issue of bonus. These guidelines evolved four important tests, whose technical and operative details are described later, to evaluate the viability of bonus proposal. They are: 1. residual reserves test; 2. yield test/profitability test; 3. time lag test; and 4. maximum permissible amount. The other guidelines are either substantiation of the parameters that are considered for these tests or are related to the procedural aspects. As has already been mentioned these guidelines have been revised from time to time keeping in view the changes that have come up in the economy in general and the changes in expectations on the role and rhyme of the Indian corporate sector. Bonus experiences of established companies and consequential difficulties had also been taken into account in the revision of guidelines from time to time.

The period around mid 70s witnessed an unmanageable inflation. This forced the government to announce several restrictive measures including the dividend freeze of 1974. The bonus guidelines were also modified with effect from July 1974. These modifications related to time lag between two successive issues which was raised from 18 months to 40 months and also to the eligibility lead-in time after stock exchange listing which was raised from 12 months to 36 months. In September, 1974 a further modification stipulated that the amount of free reserves to be capitalised should not exceed the paid up capital of the company at the time of the bonus issue. However, in July, 1975 the government liberalised the condition with regard to the paid-up capital ceiling for those of the FERA companies which were reducing the foreign shareholdings and were wanting to finance approved schemes of expansion and diversification.

The Dividend Restriction Ordinance restricting the corporate dividends had the effect as expected of depression in the stock market. It was soon realised that such a state of the capital market is likely to inhibit growth and capital formation. Consequently the government came out with a series of measures in November, 1975. According to these the time interval between two successive bonus issues was reduced from 40 months to 24 months and the time lag for submitting an application after stock exchange listing was brought down from 36 months to 12 months.

With the revision of the Companies Transfer of Profits to Reserves Rules in July 1976 a company issuing bonus shares was allowed to capitalise reserves only if it could ensure the maintenance of quantum of dividend equivalent to the average of preceding three years.

A Finance Ministry notification dated 6-6-1977 imposed a condition on a company desiring to issue bonus shares that it should submit a certificate from its auditors stating that: 1. a provision for depreciation as allowable under Income Tax Act, 1961 has adequately been made in the accounts of the company and 2. adequate provision for deferred taxation liability arising out of a change in the method of depreciation has also been provided.

The existing bonus guidelines were reviewed and revised as per notification dated 18-8-1981. The changes introduced with this revision were as follows: 1. the residual reserves as a percentage of post-bonus paid up capital was raised from 33.3% to 40%, 2. the yield criterion was raised from 9% to 10%, 3. the time lag between two successive bonus issues was raised from 24 months to 36 months and time lag between the date of application for bonus issues and the date of announcement by 'Board' was not to be more than 30 days.

In view of the difficulties experienced by the companies in submitting the General Body Resolution along with the application for issue of bonus shares, the government decided in April, 1987 that the companies can make the application within 45 days from the date of announcement of bonus issue by the 'Board' instead of 30 days. This requirement of specifying the time lag between the announcement and application to CCI was aimed to prevent unscrupulous announcements being made and the market being misled.

The time lag between two successive bonus issues had been reduced from 36 months to 24 months in 1987. A recent modification announced in February, 1990 has further reduced it to 12 months. This modification is expected to increase the frequency of bonus issues in India and companies might also maintain a regular track record of bonus offerings to their shareholders.

Bonus Guidelines

The aforesaid discussion provides a summary of modifications to the bonus guidelines in order of the dates on which they were announced. This section provides a snap view of the current state of these guidelines to date. As of February, 1990 the position stands as follows:

1. There should be a provision in the articles of association of the company for capitalisation of reserves. If not, the company should produce a resolution passed at the General Body making provisions in the Articles of Association for capitalisation.

2. Consequent to the issue of bonus shares if the subscribed and paid-up capital exceeds the authorised capital, a resolution passed at the General Body meeting in respect of increase in the authorised capital is necessary.

3. The company should furnish a resolution passed at General Body Meeting for bonus issue before an application is made to the CCI. In the General Body resolution the management's intention regarding the rate of dividend to be declared in the year immediately after the bonus issue should be indicated.

4. The bonus issue is permitted to be made out of free reserves built out of the genuine profits or share premium collected in cash only.

5. Reserves created by revaluation of fixed assets are not permitted to be capitalised.

6. Development rebate reserve/investment allowance reserve is considered as free reserve for the purpose of calculation of residual reserves test.

7. All contingent liabilities disclosed in the audited accounts which have a bearing on the net profits, shall be taken into account in the calculation of the minimum residual reserves.

8. The residual reserves after the proposed capitalisation should be at least 40 per cent of the increased paid-up capital.

9. 30 per cent of the average profits before tax of the campany for the previous three years should yield a rate of dividend on the expanded capital base of the company at 10 per cent.

10. Declaration of bonus issue in lieu of dividend is not allowed.

11. The company may make a further application for issue of bonus shares only after 12 months from the date of sanction by the government of an earlier bonus issue, if any.

12. Bonus issues are not permitted unless the partly paid shares, if any existing, are made fully paid-up.

13. No bonus issue will be permitted if there is sufficient reason to believe that the company has defaulted in respect of the payment of statutory dues of the employees such as contributory provident fund, gratuity, bonus, etc.

14. Capital reserves appearing in the Balance Sheets of the companies as a result of revaluation of assets or without accrual of cash resources will neither be allowed to be capitalised nor taken into account in the computation of the residual reserves of 40 per cent for purpose of bonus issue.

15. At any one time the total amount permitted to be capitalised for issue of bonus shares out of free reserves shall not exceed the total amount of paid-up equity capital of the company.

16. Applications for issue of bonus shares should be made within 45 days of the bonus announcement by the board of directors of the company.

17. In cases where there is any default in the payment of any term loans outstanding to any public financial institution, a no objection letter from that institution in respect of the issue of the bonus shares should be furnished by the companies concerned with the bonus issue application.

What Constitute 'Free Reserves'?

Though the guidelines cover most considerations required to evaluate a 'bonus candidate' they leave certain critical concepts inadequately clarified. For example the term 'free reserves' has been defined to exclude the share premium not collected in cash and notional revaluation reserves. From this it is not immediately clear that the cash profits realised on actual sale of assets will be available for capitalisation or not. Again the reserves can be either capital or revenue reserves from accounting point of view. Of these, revenue reserves are obviously appropriations from profits but some of the capital reserves like the capital redemption reserve are also similar appropriations. The point of contention is whether such capital reserves will form part of free reserves for capitalisation purpose? Schedule-VI to the Companies Act, 1956 defines, negatively, that reserves shall not include any amount written off or retained by way of providing for depreciation, renewals or diminution in value of assets or retained by way of providing for any known liability. It can be argued that capital reserves not earmarked for any specific purpose would be available for capitalisation as free reserves. The legal position supports this argument both negatively and positively. For example Section 2(d) of the Companies Acceptance of Deposits Rules, 1975 which lays down the limits within which a company may accept deposits from public considers capital reserves retained for any general purpose as 'free reserves'. Further, Clause 7(1) (c) under part III of Schedule-VI of Companies Act, 1956 states that the expression capital reserves shall not include any amount which is considered 'free' for distribution purposes through the Profit and Loss Account. This particular interpretation substantially widens the scope of the term 'free reserves' and impliedly permits all reserves and surpluses of a capital nature not earmarked for distribution purposes as being available for issue of bonus shares. The same Schedule defines the term negatively that it will not include any amount written off or retained for the purposes of providing for depreciation, diminution or renewals in the value of assets or even retained by way of providing for any known liability. This implies that depreciation provision and capital redemption reserves and similar such provisions will neither form part of such reserves nor be available for capitalisation. In fact, this particular definition makes an attempt to distinguish a provision from a reserve so that the general position is that while a general reserve is available for capitalisation, a provision is not. It will be seen that the debate and consequential controversies with regard to the exclusions and inclusions in the term 'free reserves' broadly centers around the following:

a) Provisions vs. Reserves.

b) General vs. Specific Reserves.

c) Capital vs. Revenue Reserves.

d) Balances in accounts like capital redemption reserves.

e) Non cash vs. Cash accumulations in capital surpluses.

The guidelines follow differentiated logic for including certain items of reserves for capitalisation and for consummating residual reserves position. For example the Investment Allowance or Development Rebate Reserve would form part of residual reserves but not for capitalisation. The differential treatment is not immediately clear. It appears the concept outlined in Schedule VI in connection with depreciation provision etc., has been employed in the case of Investment Allowance and Development Rebate also by treating them as provisions. While this clarifies the position that all provisions will not be available for capitalisation it opens up another question why provisions or reserves treated as provisions form part of residual reserves. In fact, reserves are a pool and a part of this pool is used through capitalisation for issuing bonus shares and the remainder is left as a safety cushion. One wonders if the use of the provision and the reserve of the same pool could be different.

It is time that the term 'free reserves' and its constituents must be specified very clearly either in the guidelines or through amendments in the Capital Issues (Control) Act, 1947 or the Capital Issues (Exemption) Order, 1969. The current state of the term free reserves appears to be reserve without encumbrance and a specification of the constituents of such reserves will be a function partly of corporate discretion and partly of official discreation. The guidelines could afford to be more specific on this issue to set at rest both academic and practical misgivings about it. It is suggested that the following components be considered as free reserves both for determining the eligibility for capitalisation and for reckoning the residual reserves position.

1. Share Premium realised in cash.
2. Development Rebate Reserve/Investment Allowance Reserves.
3. Accumulated Profits.
4. General Reserves and
5. Capital Reserves not retained for any specific purpose other than those created as a result of revaluation of assets and without accrual of cash resources.
6. Balance in the Sinking Fund Reserve for redemption of debentures after the redemption of such debentures.
7. Balance in Capital Redemption Reserve for redemption of redeemable preference shares after the redemption of such preference shares.

Conversely, these will be the reserves considered for residual reserves test also.

Determining the Quantum of Bonus

Having analysed the key parameter i.e., 'free reserves' that determines the eligibility of the company to issue bonus shares, we now make an endeavour to illustrate the process of determining the quantum of reserves that can be capitalised at any point of time. In other words, this is the quantum of bonus. The three relevant guidelines impinging upon this aspect are:

1. At any point of time a company is permitted an amount of not more than its paid-up capital to be capitalised out of reserves. We call this as the paid-up capital test [PCT].

2. The post-bonus reserves must be equivalent to or more than 40 percent of the post bonus paid-up capital. This test is known as residual reserves test [RRT].

3. 30 percent of the average pre-tax profits of the immediately preceding three years must be equivalent to 10 per cent of the post bonus paid-up capital. This is the yield test [YT].

To translate the guidelines into mathematical form let us consider the following notations:

P = Pre bonus paid-up capital

B = Bonus rate

FR = Free Reserves

I_1, I_2, I_3 = Profit before tax [PBT] of the three immediately preceding years and aggregate of three years' PBI=ΣI.

Using the notations

Bonus quantum	= PB
Post-bonus paid-up capital	= P[1 + B]
Post-bonus Free reserves	= [FR - PB]
Mean PBT of three preceding years	= [ΣI/3]

Using the aforesaid notations and the relevant guideiines following test equations emerge:

1. PC Test:

$P \geq PB$

2. RR Test:

$40\%P[1+B] \geq [FR-PB]$

3. Y Test:

$10\%P[1+b] \geq 30\%[\Sigma\, 1/3]$

The maximum permissible amounts allowed to be capitalised under these tests will be equal to:

1. Under PC Test:

$P = PB$

2. Under RR Test:

   40%P[1+B] = [FR-PB]

   = 1.4PB = [FR - 0.4P]

   = 7PB = [5FR -2P]

   PB = [(5FR - 2P)/7]

3. Under Y Test:

   10%P[1+B] = 30%[Σ I/3]

   = 0.1P + 0.1PB = .1 Σ I

   PB = [Σ I - P]

To illustrate numerically consider the following Net Worth Structure:

Paid-up capital	= Rs. 210 Lakhs
Free Reserves	= Rs. 140 Lakhs
Networth	= Rs. 350 Lakhs

Let the Profit Before Tax [PBT] for three years immediately preceding bonus year be Rs. 120 lakhs, Rs. 150 lakhs, and Rs. 175 lakhs respectively.

As per the above conditions the maximum amounts of reserves that can be capitalised under each of the guidelines are:

1. under PCT : Rs. 210 Lakhs.
2. under RRT : [{(5 x 140) - (2 x 210)}/7] = Rs. 40 Lakhs.
3. under YT : [(120 + 150 + 175) - 210] = Rs. 135 Lakhs.

The company will be permitted to capitalise least of the above amounts. So it can make a proposal to capitalise Rs. 40 lakhs.

Residual reserves after capitalisation of Rs. 40 lakhs will be Rs. 100 lakhs and post-bonus paid up capital will be Rs. 260 lakhs. The condition that the residual reserves must be 40 per cent of the post-bonus paid-up capital is thus satisfied since [0.4 x 250] = 100.

The yield test will allow the company to capitalise Rs. 135 lakhs. Suppose it capitalised the same amount then the post-bonus paid-up capital will be Rs. 345 lakhs and 10 per cent of this amount viz., Rs. 34.5 lakhs will be just equivalent to the 30 per cent of [345/3].

To gain a better understanding of the implications of these tests let us simulate three situations where 1. the paid-up capital is substantially less than the accumulated free reserves and the aggregate PBT for the immediately preceding three years; 2. the aggregate PBT is not very significant; and 3.

where accumulated free reserves are not very significant. Applying the three tests the quantum of bonus and the bonus rate are shown in Table - 2.2.

Because the company, in case A, has not expanded its paid-up capital base it was restricted to capitalise reserves to the extent of 100 per cent of its paid-up capital even though the three year aggregate PBT and accumulated free reserves position is very comfortable. In case B the company had a poor porfit earnings during the last three years which restricted it to capitalise only to the extent of 50 per cent of the paid-up capital in spite of a better position with regard to the accumulated free reserves and paid-up capital. As far as case C is concerned the company's free reserves constrained the capitalisation capability of the company.

Table - 2.2

Tests for Bonus Quantum Determination - A Simulation

		(Rs. In Lakhs)		
		A	B	C
I.	Particulars:			
	Paid-Up Capital	140	140	140
	Free reserves	420	420	210
	3 years aggregate PBT	560	210	560
II.	Test Results:			
	PCT	140	140	140
	YT	420	70	420
	RRT	260	260	110
III.	Bonus Quantum:	140	70	110
IV.	Bonus Rate	100%	50%	78.5%

This makes it clear that these three tests rigorously analyse the financial soundness of the company in the context of bonus issues. Also, this brings out a point that the companies need to take a balanced and cautious policy with respect to expanding the paid up capital base and the retention policy. Rather a well coordinated and integrated approach is a must especially in the area of retention policy since RRT appears to be more sensitive than the other tests in the process of determining the quantum of bonus.

Procedure Relating to Issue of Bonus Shares

CCI will consider the application for bonus by the company and approval is given adhering to the guidelines. Following the approval granted by the CCI the company has to take necessary steps for allotment of bonus shares. The steps involved are:

i. Convene a 'Board' meeting and fix the date for closure of books to ascertain the shareholders entitled for bonus shares.

ii. Issue public notice regarding closure of members' register.

iii. Intimate stock exchanges and obtain their approval for the procedure to be followed for allotment of shares.

iv. Obtain Reserve Bank of India's approval for allotment to non-residents.

v. Issue scrips/fractional certificates.

vi. File Return of Allotment with the Registrar of Companies.

VIII. Law Relating to Taxation of Bonus Shares

How are the bonus shares in the hands of the receivers i.e., shareholders, treated for tax purposes? The first question related to this will be that whether bonus shares fall within the definition of dividends under the Income Tax Act, 1961. The dividend is an inclusive term under Section 2(22) of the Act. According to this section dividend includes any distribution by a company of its accumulated porfits whether capitalised or not, if such distribution entails a release by the company to its shareholders of all or any part of the assets of the company. This implies that since issue of bonus shares does not entail a release of any of the company's assets it cannot be treated as dividends. Through issue of bonus shares the company merely confers a formal title to a proportion of accumulated profits if and when a general distribution takes place as in the event of winding-up.

This raises a collateral question that if bonus shares are not falling within the definition of dividends and are not treated as a revenue receipt, can they be accounted as capital receipts? The Supreme Court has already established in its judgment in *CIT vs. Dalmia Investments Co. Ltd., [52 ITR 567*] that bonus shares are capital receipts and not revenue receipts and therefore, cannot be taxed as income. It may be mentioned that in *Madura Mills Co. Ltd., vs. CIT [86 ITR 467*] and *D.M. Dahanukar vs. CIT [88 ITR 454*] it was held that the principle of *Dalmia* case would apply irrespective of the fact that whether the assessee is a dealer or an investor. This means even in the case where bonus shares are held as stock in trade, this should be regarded as capital asset unless the conduct of the assessee shows that he converted them as stock in trade. In *Kishore Trading Co. Ltd., vs. CIT [138 ITR 527*] the Calcutta High Court held that if an assessee is a dealer in shares, then the method of averaging would be applicable in valuing the bonus shares even if bonus shares are valued in closing stock at 'nil'.

If bonus shares are capital receipts a related question is: what their cost is? The Supreme Court in *Dalmia* case observed that there were four methods to determine the cost of bonus shares:

1. The cost can be taken to be equivalent to their face value.
2. It can be taken at 'nil' because the shareholder pays nothing for the shares.
3. The cost of the original shares can be spread over the original as well as bonus shares taken collectively and the average price found out.
4. The fall in price of the original shares on the stock exchange after the issue of bonus shares could be ascertained and this could be attributed to bonus shares.

The court also held that the third method was the proper method to value bonus shares. The court further observed that this method would be applicable only if shares rank *pari passu*. If they did not, then the cost may have to be adjusted either in proportion of face value they bear or on equitable considerations based on market price before and after the issue of bonus shares.

However, this judgment can be applied only to value the bonus shares and will not be applicable to the valuation of original shares in view of the provisions of Section 48 and 55(2) of the Income Tax Act, 1961. As per Section 55(2) the original shares will have to be valued in respect of shares acquired before 1.1.1964 either at their cost of acquisition or the market value as on that date at the option of the assessee. In *Shekhawati General Traders Ltd., vs. ITO [82 ITR 788]* the Supreme Court observed that any bonus shares or right shares issue subsequent to 1.1.1964 would be wholly extraneous and irrelevant in the valuation of original shares and not to be taken into consideration. What will be the treatment if bonus shares are received after 1.1.1964? It is interpreted, in view of the language of Section 55(2) (1) of Income Tax Act, 1961, that the assessee is entitled to take the market value as on 1.1.1964 even in respect of bonus shares. At the same time under the provisions of Section 55(2) it will be open to the assessee to either adopt the cost of acquisition as per the average method or take the fair market value as on 1.1.1964 for the valuation of bonus shares. In the case of *Emerald vs. CIT [36 ITR 257]* the Supreme Court decided that when an assessee sells his shares which had been purchased by him and retained bonus shares allocated subsequently, the profit or loss should be computed by deducting full purchase price of the original shares from the sale price ignoring bonus shares altogether. This, however, is contrary to the decision taken by Supreme Court in the case of *Dalmia*

Investment Co, where the average price was taken for computation of capital gains. The correct view on this point has been laid down in *Sutlej Cotton Mills Ltd., vs. CIT [119 ITR 666]* where the Calcutta High Court held that subsequent issue of bonus shares does not affect, alter or dilute the cost of acquisition of the original shares. In view of sections 48 and 55(2) the purchase price of shares would never change regardless of any number of bonus shares. A similar view was expressed by the Calcutta High Court in *Smt. Protima Roy vs. CIT [138 ITR 536]* where the court held that the costing of acquisition must be done in terms of sections 48 and 55(2). Deflation or inflation of the value of shares by subsequent events would not alter the original cost to the assessee. Hence, issue of bonus shares would not decrease the cost of acquisition of original shares for the purpose of computation of capital gains on the sale of such shares. Thus what fluctuates is only the value of bonus shares, but the purchase price of the original shares cannot and does not change.[11]

Notes and References

1. The power to pay dividends is inherent in every company, and therefore, it need not be given by the Memorandum or Articles. But the directors may refuse to exercise this power and in that event the shareholders cannot insist on the payment of dividends even if the profits are very large unless the directors fraudulently decline them [Band vs. Barrow Haematite Co. (1902) 1 Ch. 353]. Where they chose to exercise the power, they are required by Section 217 of the Companies Act, 1956 to state in their report to be attached to the company's Balance Sheet the amount which they recommend should be paid by way of dividend. Then, regulation 85 of Table-A in the First Schedule to the Act stipulates that the company in the 'AGM' may declare the dividend which should in no event exceed the amount recommended by the directors in their report.
2. The Companies [Transfer to Reserves] Rules, 1975 provide that before dividend declaration a percentage of profits as specified below should be transfered to the reserves of the company.

Table - 2.R

Transfer of Reserves Required for a Proposed Dividend Rate

Proposed dividend [D] as a percentage of paid-up capital	Amount to be transfered to reserves as a percentage of paid-up capital
$10.0 < D < 12.5$	2.5
$12.5 \leq D < 15.0$	5.0
$15.0 \leq D < 20.0$	7.5
$D \geq 20.0$	10.0

3. In the literature on corporate dividend policies, there are two strands of thought with regard to the relative importance that the dividend decision has in the financial policy of a company. Some consider dividend decision as an active policy variable [Lintner] while others maintain

that dividend payment is passive residual after the decision about retained earnings has been made [Walter, James and M.M.,]. But the sum and substance of their studies indicate that the decision to retain profits by those companies pursuing vigrously to maximise the wealth of the shareholders has over whelming support of the shareholders.

4. Benjamin Graham and David Dodd: 'Security Analysis-Principles and Techniques', McGraw Hill Book Co., 1951. pp. 440.

5. Henry E. Hogland: 'Corporate Finance', McGraw Hill Book Co., 1947. pp. 578.

6. For a complete case refer to "ACC Turmoil on Stock Exchange-What Role Financial Institutions" by Kumaran Pola as a cover story to Commerce, November 17, 1984. pp. 784-799.

7. News report in the Economic Times, 14-16 July, 1988.

8. Gupta, L.C., "Bonus Shares: Facts, Fiction and Policy", Chartered Accountant, Vol. XXVII, No. 2, August, 1978.

9. Mark S. Grinblatt, Ronald W. Masulis and Sheridan Titman: "The Valuation Effects of Stock Splits and Stock Dividends", Journal of Financial Economics, 13 [1984]. pp. 464.

10. Dolley, J.C., "Common Stock Split Up - Motives and Effects", Harvard Business Review, October, 1933. pp. 70-81.

11. Refer for details Arvind P. Datar: "Valuation of Bonus Shares", Chartered Secretary, March 1985. pp. 156-158.

III

Bonus Shares - An Empirical Retrospect

I. Introduction

The purpose of this chapter is to describe the characteristic features of bonus shares issued during the period 1977-88.

An analysis of pre-1971 bonus share issues by Gupta revealed that the Indian companies have no consistent policy with respect to the frequency of bonus issues. Also there is no definite policy of any individual firm with regard to the interval between two successive bonus issues. These conclusions were noted by Gupta with regard to the bonus issues made before coming into effect of the bonus guidelines that provided a mandate with regard to time interval between two successive bonus issues. It is noteworthy to observe if there is any marked shift in this trend during post-1971 period. Therefore, we specifically address our analysis to throw light on several aspects of corporate policies and practices regarding bonus issues such as bonus ratios, frequency and regularity of such issues by individual companies and the relation of bonus issues to the size of the companies.

The Bombay Stock Exchange Directory provides complete information with regard to changes in capital structure of all listed companies along with the year, nature and amount of such changes. The capital structure chronology of listed companies therefore contains the timing and quantum of increase in the paid up capital *via* transfer from reserves through bonus issues. We have used this basic information for our empirical analysis in this chapter. The BSE Directory updated to June, 1989 provided information for 435 bonus issues made by 259 companies during our period of study. As already noted in Chapter-I we have taken the year of bonus issue as the one in which bonus shares are actually allotted and transfer of reserves to capital account has taken place. Companies that have given bonus shares during the study period have been presented in Industry Group on the basis of BSE classification only.

Section two deals with the number of bonus issues. It also analyses the frequency of bonus issues made by the same company during the period of study. The time interval between two successive bonus issues is also presented in this section. Section three analyses the bonus ratios during the period of study, identifies the more popular bonus ratios and gives the industry composition of bonus issues. Section four tabulates information about the amount of bonus issues and analyses this facet with an industry wise breakdown. Section five presents data on size of bonus issues and analyses the size of the companies issuing bonus to delineate the bonus record of different size groups of companies. Section six provides an analysis of the extent of capitalisation over time and industry groups and also presents the position of residual reserves for the study period. The last section summarises the conclusions emerging from the empirical data analysis in this chapter.

II. Number of Bonus Issues

Table - 3.1 is a two-way matrix presenting the data relating to the bonus issues of our sample companies according to the year and industry origin of issue. It covers 435 bonus issues made by 259 companies belonging to 19 industry groups during a period of 12 years. Of the 435 bonus issues, Engineering firms alone account for 90 i.e. 20.6% and are highest distributors of bonus. It will be noticed that this group performed well in the years 1981, 1982, 1986 and 1987. There were 50 bonus issues, almost a quantum jump, in 1982 of which 15 were by Engineering Industry. An important factor which pushed up the number of bonus issues in 1982 appears to be the modified guidelines announced in 1981 whose full effect was reached in 1982. The number of issues being in the range of five to seven over the period, these four years are the super average years for the industry. A glance on number of issues in different years reveals that 1987 has been the star performer accounting for 57 issues out of a total of 435 issues i.e. around 13% of the total issues. A close examination of the table reveals that 35% of the total bonus issues are made during 1985-87 the period which is roughly synchronous with the capital market boom. As a consequence of the relaxation in bonus issue guidelines for profit-making-closely held companies enforced in March, 1985, many such companies announced bonus shares either before the public issue or after opening of public issue to their promoters and associates and there had been a raise in the number of bonus issues made during 1985-87.

Distribution of companies according to frequency of bonus issues made by the same company during 1977-88 is given in Table - 3.2. Of the 259 companies issuing a total of 435 bonus issues, 130 companies came out with just one issue during the whole of 12 year period. It will be noticed that only five companies could make bonus issues at the rate of 4 issues for 12 years, i.e., maximum permissible statutory gap of 3 years between two successive bonus issues. These companies are:

a. Century Enka

b. Chloride India

c. Indian Oxygen

d. Kirlosker Cummins

f. Supreme Industries

Table - 3.1

Bonus Issues Made By Different Industries During 1977-88

Years/Industry	1977	'78	'79	'80	'81	'82	'83	'84	'85	'86	'87	'88	Total
Trading	0	0	0	0	0	0	0	0	0	0	1	0	1
Transport	0	0	0	0	0	1	0	0	0	0	0	0	1
Elec. Generation	0	0	0	0	1	0	0	0	0	0	1	0	2
Potteries & Tiles	0	0	0	1	0	1	0	0	0	0	0	0	2
Cement	0	0	1	0	0	0	0	0	1	0	1	0	3
Banking & Insurance	1	0	1	0	1	0	0	0	1	0	0	0	4
Coal & Mining	1	0	0	1	0	0	0	0	1	0	1	0	4
Jute Textiles	0	0	0	1	1	0	0	0	1	2	0	0	5
Paper & Paper Products	1	1	0	1	0	1	0	1	0	1	2	0	8
Sugar & Breweries	0	0	0	0	0	3	1	0	2	1	2	0	9
Food Products	0	0	1	2	0	1	2	0	5	1	2	5	19
Silk & Woolen Textiles	1	1	2	3	1	3	2	2	2	1	0	4	22
Metals	2	2	1	0	3	2	5	0	4	1	0	3	23
Elec. Equipment	2	1	3	2	3	4	2	2	3	1	7	1	31
Cotton Textiles	4	3	3	6	4	3	4	1	0	3	3	1	35
Plantation	3	6	1	3	1	2	0	1	11	4	7	1	40
Chemicals	5	5	7	6	3	4	2	10	3	8	11	4	68
Others	2	5	3	4	5	10	8	1	8	8	10	4	68
Engineering	6	6	4	6	8	15	6	5	7	15	8	4	90
Total No.	28	30	27	36	31	50	32	23	49	46	56	27	435

On an average per company bonus issue works out to 1.7 [435/259] over the twelve year period and one bonus for every seven years [12/1.79]. A little less than half of the companies have issued bonus shares more than once during the study period [for industry wise number of companies and frequency of bonus issues see Table - 3.2A]. The mean number of bonus issues of companies issuing two or more bonus issues works out to 2.36 [(174+111+20)/(87+37+5)].

Table - 3.2

Frequency of Bonus Issues Made By the Same Company During 1977-88

No. of Bonus Issues Made	Companies		Bonus Issues	
	No.	%	No.	%
One	130	50.19	130	29.89
Two	87	33.59	174	40.00
Three	37	14.29	111	25.52
Four	5	1.93	20	4.60
Total	259	100.00	435	100.00

The time interval presented in Table - 3.3 is measured between two successive bonus issues made by the same company during the 12 year period. In so doing the first issue by all such companies will be counted out. Such an exclusion will reduce the total number of bonus issues as shown in the second column of the table to 176. It may be recalled that of the total number of bonus issues covered in this study i.e., 435, 130 issues are excluded because they are not followed by any successive issue during the period of study. Of the remaining 305 issues another 129 are excluded being the first issue and thus being the time reference point for measuring the interval between the first two successive bonus issues. The second successive issue is both a reference point for measuring the interval of the third successive issue and also a destination time point for measuring the time interval between the first and second issues. For example consider a company issuing three bonus issues in 1979, 1982 and 1985. In this case the time interval between the first and second issues will be three years (1982-1979) and the interval between the next two issues again will be three years (1985-1982). It is obvious that for three issues only two intervals are counted because of the first issue in 1979 is the initial reference point and the second issue in 1982 is a reference point for the second interval of three years and a destination point for the computation of initial time interval of three years. All figures in Table-3.3 have been derived in a similar manner.

Table - 3.2A

Number of Bonus Issues Made By Companies - An Industry Classification

Indusry	Number of bonus issues by each company					
	One	Two	Three	Four	No.of companies	No. of bonus issues
Banking & Insurance	0	2	0	0	2	4
Metals	13	5	0	0	18	23
Elect. Generation	2	0	0	0	2	2
Trading	1	0	0	0	1	1
Transport	1	0	0	0	1	1
Coal & Mining	1	0	1	0	2	4
Cement	1	1	0	0	2	3
Potteries & Tiles	2	0	0	0	2	2
Cotton Text	10	11	1	0	22	35
Jute Text	3	1	0	0	4	5
Silk & Woolen Text	8	2	2	1	13	22
Paper & Paper Products	4	2	0	0	6	8
Elec. Equip	10	4	3	1	18	31
Engineering	18	22	8	1	49	90
Chemicals	15	16	7	0	38	68
Sugar & Breweries	7	1	0	0	8	9
Food Products	4	3	3	0	10	19
Plantations	7	9	5	0	21	40
Others	23	8	7	2	40	68
Total	130	87	37	5	259	435

It is gathered from Table - 3.3 that 13 bonus issues had a time interval of two years, even though the minimum statutory time gap is three years. It must be noted that all these issues relate to pre 1980 when the guideline relating to the minimum gap was only 24 months. The largest number of issues i.e., 52 has a time interval of three years.

Table - 3.3

Time Interval Between Two Successive Bonus Issues Made During 1977-88

Time Interval in Years	Bonus Issues	
	No.	%
2	13	7.39
3	52	29.55
4	41	23.30
5	23	13.07
6	21	11.93
7	8	4.55
8	8	4.55
9	4	2.27
10	4	2.27
11	1	0.57
12	1	0.57
Total	176	100.00

This combined with 41 issues with a time interval of four years yields the model number of bonus issues for the series. In other words the time range 3-4 years was the most popular range accounting for 53% [(52+41)/176]. The time interval ranging from 7-12 years has been less known as there were only 26 issues in all within this range. The distribution pattern of time interval underlines the corporate decision makers keenness to implement the bonus guidelines with regard to mandatory time gap. Since the number of issues decreases as the time interval increases corporate bonus decisions appeared to be tilted more towards a narrower time gap than a larger time gap.

Though it is obvious that the frequency of bonus issues by the Indian corporate sector has shown no regularity of time pattern across the bonus issues covered, majority, nevertheless, of the issues seemed to have been issued with a 'rhythmic' periodicity. The non-rhythmic nature of bonus issue by other companies, however, need not necessarily be interpreted as companies not having a policy with respect to the bonus issues. They do have some policies with regard to issue of bonus. These policies relate not to the periodicity but to more fundamental variables like the maintainability of the earnings, dividends etc., as has been revealed by the 'Capital Market' study. Should we expect a rigidly defined and spelled out periodicity of bonus issues by the companies, the equity is relinquished of its nature.

III. Bonus Ratios

A bonus ratio is an important element of market intelligence and is at the same time a very critical decision variable in the disposition of net surplus and accumulated reserves by a company. It is not generally a random decision and a careful arithmetic with regard to the future implications goes into it. On an aggregative plane it is interesting to observe the patterns of these ratios over time and identifying some of the more popular bonus ratios. Table - 3.4 and Table - 3.5 consummate these objectives. The industry distribution of bonus ratios also sheds light on the bonus performance of companies. Industry distribution of the bonus ratios will naturally show a diversity among firms because of the absence of an industry wide pattern.

Table - 3.4

Bonus Ratios During 1977-88

Ratios	1.1	1:2	1:3	1:4	1:5	2:3	2:5	3:5	4:5	Others	Total	
Year											No.	%
1977	5	11	0	3	1	0	1	5	0	2	28	6.44
1978	6	8	4	3	1	0	1	3	1	3	30	6.90
1979	5	5	5	3	2	0	1	3	0	3	27	6.21
1980	10	7	3	8	5	0	1	2	0	0	36	8.28
1981	7	9	4	0	2	0	3	3	1	2	31	7.13
1982	6	14	6	2	2	3	6	7	1	3	50	11.49
1983	11	3	2	1	0	1	3	7	2	2	32	7.36
1984	7	2	0	2	3	1	3	3	1	1	23	5.29
1985	17	10	5	4	1	1	5	2	1	3	49	11.26
1986	23	9	2	1	2	1	4	3	1	0	46	10.57
1987	21	12	3	1	2	1	8	7	0	1	56	12.87
1988	8	6	1	1	0	1	5	3	2	0	27	6.21
Total	126	96	35	29	21	9	41	48	10	20	435	100.00
%	28.97	22.07	8.05	6.67	4.83	2.07	9.43	11.03	2.30	4.60	100.00	

Table - 3.5

Popular Bonus Ratios

(In Percentage)

Ratio	1977-82	1983-88	Total
1:1	19.31	37.34	28.97
1:2	26.73	18.03	22.07
3:5	11.39	10.73	11.03
2:5	6.93	12.02	9.43
Others	35.64	21.88	28.50
Total	100.00	100.00	100.00

The time distribution of bonus ratios shown in Table - 3.4 brings out clearly the greatest significance of the 1:1 ratio followed by 1:2 ratio. The ratio 3:5 also appears to be adoptive on a fairly large scale by companies. Thus, as many as 126 issues during the 12 year period have a 1:1 ratio, 96 issues were based on 1:2 ratio and 48 issues were based on 3:5 ratio. And these ratios are also the ratios rated in order of importance. It is interesting to note that the largest number of issues in any single period were based on 1:1 ratio. There were 23 issues in 1986, and 21 issues in 1987 in the ratio of 1:1. It may again be explained that the ratio 1:1 is a ceiling which guidelines of 1981 provide and which continues operative to date except for certain selective official waivers. It may be observed that the predominance of high bonus ratios 1:1, 1:2 does underline the corporate propensity to capitalise within the maximum permissible limits.

Table - 3.5 throws further light on corporate adoption of certain bonus ratios during the period of study. Data in this table has been split into two time periods viz., 1977-82 [that is the period before the major revision of guidelines has shown its full effect] and 1983-88 [the post revision of guidelines period]. The table confirms the observations made in the preceding part with respect to most popular bonus ratios. It may be noted that most popular bonus ratio 1:1 got a real thrust after the enforcement of the revised guidelines. The percentage share of this ratio in all issuings increased from 19.31 per cent in the first period to 37.34 per cent in the second period. It is some what intriguing to note that the ratio 1:2 suffered a set back in its relative importance in the second period. Its percentage share came down heavily from 26.73 per cent to 18.03 per cent. It is therefore, a ratio which though still popular appears to be witnessing a declining popularity. The ratio 2:5 has gained in popularity by around 100 per cent over the two time periods studied. As already noted these trends are mere patterns and companies individually will be doing a hard exercise about their financing before announcing a particular bonus ratio. It may even be suggested that the bonus ratio patterns serve to delineate the broadly structured financial patterns of firms falling as a group within a particular bonus ratio range. May be all such firms have a given strength in terms of reserves and it is not inconceivable that their past and expected profit performance are also almost identical. The point being made out here is that firms which belong to a given bonus ratio range are also the firms which belong to a homogeneous financial structure class.

Table - 3.6 presents the industry-wise distribution of different bonus ratios. It may be noted that the popularity of 1:1 ratio is not shared by all industry groups alike. It appears to be a favourate of Engineering firms followed by Chemicals group. Both account for 35 and 13 issues respectively.

The next best ratio 1:2 again happens to be a highly popular ratio for Engineering and Chemical industries in that order. Chemical companies appear to be almost equally divided in terms of number of bonus issues over the ratios 1:1 [13], 1:2 [12]. It is interesting to note that 70 per cent of total issues [305/435] are accounted by the ratios 1:1, 1:2, 2:5 and 3:5. Table - 3.5 has already brought the popularity pattern of these ratios out. Thus, these ratios rank as the most favoured ratios both in over all time interval and in terms of the industry wide distribution as well.

Table - 3.6 highlights some of the more popular bonus ratios for specific industry groups. There are seven issues out of a total of 23 issues made by firms belonging to Metal industry in the ratio of 1:1. This ratio is the most favoured ratio in the Jute Textiles firms. In fact, all the five issues made by the Jute industry are in the 1:1 ratio only. Cotton Textiles and Silk & Woolen Textiles were showing 1:2 as their favoured bonus ratio. Food Products favoured 1:1 ratio and Plantations weighted their preference almost equally for 1:1 and 1:2 ratios.

Table - 3.6

Bonus Ratios By Different Industries During 1977-88

Ratio / Industry	1:1	1:2	1:3	1:4	1:5	2:3	2:5	3:5	4:5	Others	Total
Banking & Insurance	1	2	0	1	0	0	0	0	0	0	4
Metals	7	4	5	3	0	0	3	1	0	0	23
Elec. Generation	0	0	1	0	1	0	0	0	0	0	2
Trading	0	0	0	0	0	0	0	1	0	0	1
Transport	0	1	0	0	0	0	0	0	0	0	1
Coal & Mining	2	0	0	1	0	0	1	0	0	0	4
Cement	1	0	0	0	1	0	0	0	0	1	3
Potteries & Tiles	0	2	0	0	0	0	0	0	0	0	2
Cotton Textiles	6	8	4	5	3	2	2	4	0	1	35
Jute Textiles	5	0	0	0	0	0	0	0	0	0	5
Silk & Woolen textiles	3	9	2	1	0	0	2	5	0	0	22
Paper & Paper Products	2	2	1	2	1	0	0	0	0	0	8
Elect. Equipment	6	5	4	2	0	1	2	6	2	3	31
Engineering	35	24	3	0	2	5	2	11	1	7	90
Chemicals	13	13	5	3	6	0	12	8	5	3	68
Sugar & Breweries	5	0	1	1	0	0	1	1	0	0	9
Food Products	8	4	0	0	0	0	4	2	0	1	19
Plantation	10	11	4	8	2	0	3	1	1	0	40
Others	22	11	5	2	5	1	9	8	1	4	68
Total	126	96	35	29	21	9	41	48	10	20	435

IV. Amount of Bonus Issues

A bonus issue can be expressed as a bonus ratio or on the aggregate plane as an average bonus ratio. This measure can be determined by dividing the total bonus amount by pre-bonus equity capital involved in all the bonus issues during a particular period. Such a measurement generally reflects the likely effect of bonus issues on the market psychology. It may be perceived as a pricing factor even though the most common price effects are measured along the bonus ratio. While the bonus ratio will have an immediate impact on the market the average bonus ratio will build up such an impact over a period of time. It may be confessed that the average bonus ratio conceals the high low ratios of a given accounting period.

Table - 3.7 provides a glimpse of the amount of the bonus and the average bonus ratio for all bonus issues for the study period of twelve years covered. It is interesting to observe that the average bonus ratio has most of the times been within a range of 45-50 per cent and suggests the average corporate propensity to distribute bonus shares. The exceptional years when this ratio has climbed its peaks are 1986 and 1987 followed by the year 1988. It may be noticed that the number of bonus issues in 1986 and 1987 also happened to be one of the largest of the period and the amount involved in all these bonus issues for the two years is also the largest forming as it does around 38 percent of the aggregate bonus amount for all the 12 years. It may be mentioned that the direct Balance Sheet impact of the high average bonus ratio would be a substantial increase in the equity capital of the company concerned, because such capital would raise on the whole by the same proportion as the average bonus ratio. For example the aggregate pre-bonus equity capital of all companies that issued 46 bonus issues during 1986 increased from a pre-bonus level of Rs. 266.98 crores to a post-bonus level of Rs. 441.23 crores, inclusive of the amount of bonus which involved a transfer of an identical sum from reserves to paid-up capital account. A similar impact is noticeable for the year 1987 when the pre-bonus equity of Rs. 314.74 crores shot up to Rs. 513 crores. An enlargement of the paid-up capital base in consequence of bonus issues and in proportion to average bonus ratio will have the effect of lowering down all the financial performance ratios based on paid-up capital and therefore, be imperative for the companies issuing bonus shares to improve their profit performance with a view to maintaining and also improving their share prices. Companies which fail to achieve this will find adverse market reactions.

Table - 3.7

Size of Bonus Issues Made During 1977-78

Year	No. of Bonus Issues	Amount of Bonus Rs. Lakhs	%	Pre Bonus Equity Rs. Lakhs	Average Bonus Ratio
1977	28	5132	5.19	10329	49.69
1978	30	2116	2.14	4330	48.87
1979	27	3756	3.80	9997	37.57
1980	36	6065	6.13	12382	48.98
1981	31	4969	5.03	10917	45.52
1982	50	7411	7.50	15643	47.38
1983	32	6712	6.79	12790	52.48
1984	23	5060	5.12	10673	47.41
1985	49	8614	8.71	17645	48.82
1986	46	17425	17.63	26698	65.27
1987	56	19828	20.06	31474	63.00
1988	27	11772	11.91	21178	55.59
Total	435	98860	100.00	184056	53.72

Table - 3.8 portrays the industry-wise distribution of total bonus amounts and the average bonus ratios for the entire study period. As can be seen from the data in Table-3.8 the star performers whose bonus ratio is more than 60 per cent are Jute textiles, Food Products and Engineering industries. The five Jute textile bonus issues which account for 1.5 per cent of the total bonus amount have achieved an average bonus ratio of a little more than 100 per cent. It may be recalled that these five jute textile issues came out only with a ratio of 1:1 [see table-3.6]. The second group of good performance within a range of 56-59.9 per cent comprised of trading [59.88%], Plantations [58.56%], Banking and Insurance [58.37%], Silk and Woolen Textiles [57.14%], and Sugar and Breweries [56.88%] in that order. Except for Engineering industry all other high performers belong to traditional industry group including Trading and Consumer goods. A surprising phenomenon is that all textiles groups capitalised their reserves at high ratio in spite of the need for funds for the replacement and modernisation of their old and obsolete plants. A possible explanation for this appears to be the desire to correct the market psychology and to take advantage of the reserves position built-up during more prosperous years starting with mid-80's. It is conceivable that some of these traditional industries have announced large bonus issues after long time internal. Electric Generation showed a tendency of conservatism in the capitalisation of reserves with an average bonus ratio of 23.14%. This is of course not without justification. Uncertainties that this industry faces are many because of its dependence on Government policies and it being public utility. To the extent reserves are capitalised ceases to be freely available funds for management, they tend to be conservative in bonus issues to meet any unforeseen contingency.

Table - 3.8

Average Bonus Ratios of Different Industries During 1977-88

Industry	No. of Bonus Issues	Bonus Amount Rs. Lakhs	%	Pre Bonus Equity Amount Rs. Lakhs	Average Bonus Ratio In %
Banking & Insurance	4	474	0.48	812	58.37
Metals	23	9347	9.45	23062	40.53
Elec. Generation	2	451	0.46	1949	23.14
Trading	1	918	0.93	1533	59.88
Transport	1	200	0.20	400	50.00
Coal & Mining	4	236	0.24	532	44.36
Cement	3	1410	1.43	6441	21.89
Potteries & Tiles	2	130	0.13	260	50.00
Cotton Textiles	35	5143	5.20	10822	47.52
Jute Textiles	5	1497	1.51	1493	100.27
Silk & Woolen Textiles	22	7662	7.75	13408	57.14
Paper & Paper Products	8	1240	1.25	2549	48.65
Elect. Equipment	31	5421	5.48	10111	53.61
Engineering	90	22551	22.81	33976	66.37
Chemicals	68	21504	21.75	40376	53.26
Sugar & Breweries	9	992	1.00	1744	56.88
Food Products	19	4644	4.70	6782	68.48
Plantation	40	4508	4.56	7698	58.56
Others	68	10532	10.65	20108	52.38
Total	435	98860	100.00	184056	53.72

Table - 3.9 presents the frequency distribution of bonus issues by sub-periods. The total period of 12 years has been split into three sub-periods, viz., 1) 1977-80, 2) 1981-84 and 3) 1985-88. The first sub-period coincides with the pre-1981 bonus guidelines. The second sub-period is immediately followed the revision of guidelines and third sub-period is coterminuous with the capital market buoyant phase. It may be noted that some modification to the guidelines were announced in the last sub-period and they compounded well with the capital market boom. The number of bonus issues has continually increased from one sub- period to other because of the push factors each succeeding sub-period associated with viz., the new guidelines of the second sub-period and capital market boom in the third sub-period. It is remarkable that the amount involved in all the bonus issues during the third sub-period was an all time high and this has been accompanied by the largest increase in the number of bonus issues as well. One would naturally expect the implication of these developments in the form of a peak average bonus ratio in the average bonus ratio of all the sub-periods taken together. It will also be noted that the annualised average bonus ratio recording a rising trend over the three successive sub-periods. Since these sub-periods comprise four years each the annualised average bonus ratio will follow the same trend as the average bonus ratio over the three sub-periods. The three annualised average bonus ratios are rising over the successive sub-period and the ratio of the third sub-period is peak.

Table -3.9

Size of Bonus Issues During Sub-Period

(Rs. in Lakhs)

Period	No. of Bonus Issues	Amount of Bonus Issues Rs.	Pre-Bonus Equity Capital Rs.	Average Bonus Rate	Annualised Bonus Rate
Upto 1980	121	17069	37038	46.09	11.52
1981-1984	136	24152	50023	48.28	12.07
After 1984	178	57639	96995	59.42	14.86
Total	435	98860	184056	53.72	12.82

The overall annualised average bonus ratio in the last column is 12.82. However, annualised average bonus ratio for the total period based on the figures given in total row is 13.43 [53.72/4] the difference is because of rounding. The figure 53.72 is obtained by dividing the total amount of bonus issues [98860] by total pre-bonus equity capital [184056]. The sub-period average bonus ratios [46.09, 48.28 and 59.42] add up to 153.79 yielding a simple average of 51.26 and the latter figure when divided by four exactly yields 12.82.

V. Bonus Quantum - A Size Wise Analysis

Under the existing bonus guidelines a company is permitted at any time to capitalise its reserves to the extent of its paid-up capital. This stipulation, thus, makes a ceiling on the quantum of bonus. It will be interesting to analyse the quantum of capitalisation by companies of different sizes. the sizes of company for our purpose is measured on the basis of pre-bonus equity paid-up capital. Table-3.10 presents a two way matrix of bonus range and company size. It can be noticed from the table that small and medium size companies dominate both in the frequency of bonus issues and in the extent of capitalisation. Bonus issues with less than Rs. 50 lakhs account for 28.51 percent [124/435] and out of these the companies with less than Rs. 100 lakhs of pre-bonus paid up capital account for a large chunk of 24.14 per cent [105/435] in the total number of bonus issues. This implies that the study period is dominated by small and medium size firms' bonus issues. This is evident from the table if we observe that 139 out of a total of 435 bonus issues, almost 1/3, are made by companies with less than Rs. 100 lakhs of pre-bonus equity paid up capital and 203 [46.67 per cent]

Table - 3.10

Number of Bonus Issues - An Analysis of Bonus Quantum and Company Size

(Rs. in Lakhs)

Bonus Range	Pre Bonus Equity Capital					Rs.			
Rs.	<100	100-200	200-300	300-400	400-500	500-1000	1000-2000	2000 and Above	Total
Below 50	105	18	1	0	0	0	0	0	124
50-100	33	35	11	4	2	0	0	0	85
100-200	0	23	27	18	10	10	0	0	88
200-300	1	0	16	5	10	8	3	0	43
300-400	0	0	0	16	0	11	5	0	32
400-500	0	0	0	0	6	6	5	1	18
500-1000	0	0	0	0	1	13	13	4	31
1000 & Above	0	0	0	0	0	0	7	7	14
Total	139	76	55	43	29	48	33	12	435

issues are made by companies with a paid-up capital range of Rs. 100-500 lakhs. Another point that strikingly appears from the table is that the quantum of bonus is less than Rs. 100 lakhs for 48.05 per cent [209/435] and that number of bonus issues with a bonus quantum of less than Rs. 500 lakhs is 89.66 per cent [390/435]. More than 2/3 of the total bonus issues are having less than Rs. 200 lakhs of amount of bonus. Our earlier observation regarding the bonus ratios may be recalled here since it is obvious from the table that the highest number of bonus issues appear at the intersection of the matrix. For example 105 bonus issues are having less than Rs. 50 lakhs as bonus quantum and were made by companies with less than Rs. 100 lakhs of pre- bonus equity paid-up capital. Thirty five issues made by companies having a paid up capital range of Rs. 100-200 lakhs are with a bonus quantum range of Rs. 50-100 lakhs. This strengthens our earlier observation that the firms favoured a very high ratio of capitalisation and their bonus behaviour reflects to be aggressive in sharing the prosperity of the company at the earliest with the shareholders.

VI. Extent of Capitalisation of Reserves

Source of bonus issues is the accumulation in free reserves and the accounting process comprises a draft on these reserves together with an identical transfer to paid-up capital account. It is easy to see that the corporate bonus behaviour has to be basically founded on the accumulation in the free reserves. In fact, the bonus guidelines insisting upon a certain minimum residual reserves position is primarily aimed to restrain companies from excessive lavishness in the issue of bonus shares for one reason or the other and to constrain them to a rational behaviour. In view of this one may exepect that the amount of bonus and the amount of free reserves are well correlated and there should be a high degree of coefficient of correlation in the variations in the two variables over time. A low degree of correlation in the direction of change of bonus amount and the direction of change in the amount of free reserves may be interpreted as sub-optimal or irrational corporate bonus behaviour. Table 3.11 measures the coefficient of concurrent correlation between the amount of bonus and the amount of free reserves. It may be noted that the coefficient of correlation is of a very high degree which supports the '*a priori*' reasoning with regard to the relationship between the two variable. It may be safely concluded that the overall corporate bonus behaviour over the 12 years period has been founded on a safe financial logic having behind a substantial safety cushion of reserves. It must, however, be conferred that the corporate sector has been displaying a measured aggressiveness in capitalising the reserves over time. It may be seen from Table - 3.11 that the amount of bonus as a percentage of capitalisation has declined from 21.46 per cent in 1977 to 15.99 per cent in 1987. This conclusion excluded 1988 since the figures for that year are only upto 31 March.

It has been stated above that the position of post-bonus reserves for the sample companies in our study has remained consistently comfortable and that this confirms the rationality of corporate bonus behaviour. Table - 3.12 bears this fact out. It will be seen that the residual reserves position has consistently been strengthening upto 1986. There has been a decline in 1987 and a peak in the post-bonus equity resulting in a substantial decline in the residual reserves percentage to equity. It will be recalled from Table-3.7 that this was an exceptional year when the number of bonus issues peaked up to 56 and average bonus ratio also was a very high at 63 per cent. This may be considered as the corporate response to market psychology which stooped to highly susceptible position because 1987 was the beginning of the dissipation of market boom which began in 1985. Many companies desiring to raise new capital wanted to play on this sweetner to attract potential investors. It may be noted that the percentage of residual reserves to equity finally was restored to 333.62 just in the first quarter of 1988. In fact, this percentage has always been more than 100 except in 1979 when it was 91.22 per cent against the statutory requirement of just 40 per cent. The vicissitudes in the percentage of residual reserves over the period of study do not reflect even for a single year inaggressiveness as revealed by the percentage of residual reserves to equity has not come any where near 40 per cent.

Table - 3.11

Extent of Capitalisation of Reserves During 1977-88

Rs. in Lakhs

Year	No. of Bonus Issues	Amount of Bonus Rs.	(+/-)	Pre-Bonus Reserve Rs.	(+/-)	% of capitalisation	Concurrences
1977	28	5132		23918		21.46	
1978	30	2116	-	8914	-	23.74	+
1979	27	3756	+	16301	+	23.04	+
1980	36	6065	+	36482	+	16.62	+
1981	31	4969	-	27050	-	18.37	+
1982	50	7411	+	51550	+	14.38	+
1983	32	6712	-	38129	-	17.60	+
1984	23	5060	-	36209	-	13.97	+
1985	49	8614	+	63888	+	13.48	+
1986	46	17425	+	168663	+	10.33	+
1987	56	19828	+	123992	-	15.99	-
1988	27	11772	-	121700	-	9.67	+
Total	435	98860		716796		13.80	

Coefficient of concurrent correlation = $\pm [\pm \{2C - N)/N]^{-2}$

Where 'C' = Number of concurrences and 'N' = Number of comparisons.

$= \pm [\pm \{2x10 - 11\}/11]^{-2} = 0.90$

Table - 3.13 presents an industry-wise distribution of the bonus amount, the pre-bonus reserves, the position of bonus amount as a percentage of reserves and also the residual reserves as a percentage of post-bonus paid-up equity capital. It will be seen that most of the industry groups where both in number of bonus issues and number of firms are high [Refer to Table - 3.2A] have obtained a low bonus percentage [amount of bonus as a percentage of pre-bonus reserves]. For example 23 bonus issues by 18 firms of the Metalindustry gave a bonus percentage of 9.39 only. Similarly the bonus percentage for

Cotton Textiles is 8.71 with 35 issues of 22 firms. The bonus percentage is also not very high in the case of Electric Equipment industry (31 issues and 18 firms) Engineering industry (90 issues of 40 firms) and Plantations (40 issues of 28 firms). In contrast this percentage is very high say in the case of Trading industry where only one issue by just one firm is included. Again, this percentage is quite high at 68.55 per cent for Banking and Insurance having four issues by two firms. Potteries and Tiles with two issues of two firms represent a high bonus percentage of 26.26. The Food Products industry is recording a high rate of bonus percentage at 29.07 with just 10 firms and 19 issues. A possible explanation for this phenomenon appears to be that the number of issues and number of firms together affect the aggregate amount of the bonus and in most of the industry groups covered in the study the pre- bonus reserves consequentially dip the bonus percentage. In other words the inter industry comparisons will be determined by the relative variations in the amount of bonus and pre-bonus reserves in any two given industry groups.

Table - 3.12

Residual Reserves as a Percentage of Post-Bonus Equity

(Rs. in Lakhs)

Year	Residual Reserves Rs.	Post Bonus Equity Rs.	Percentage of Reserves to Equity
1977	18786	15461	121.51
1978	6798	6446	105.46
1979	12545	13753	91.22
1980	30417	18447	164.89
1981	22081	15886	139.00
1982	44139	23054	191.46
1983	31417	19502	161.10
1984	31149	15733	197.99
1985	55274	26259	210.50
1986	151238	44123	342.73
1987	104164	51302	203.04
1988	109928	32950	333.62
Total	617936	282916	218.00

Table - 3.13

Extent of Capitalisation of Reserves By the Industries During 1977-88

Rs. in Lakhs

Industry	No. of Bonus Issues	Amount of Bonus Issues Rs.	Pre Bonus Reserves Rs.	Bonus as % Reserves	Residual Reserves as % Equity *
Banking & Insurance	4	474	1785	26.55	101.94
Metals	23	9347	99576	9.39	278.41
Elec. Generation	2	451	7766	5.81	304.79
Trading	1	918	3107	29.55	89.31
Transport	1	200	1576	12.69	229.33
Coal & Mining	4	236	1399	16.87	151.43
Cement	3	1410	18094	7.79	212.51
Potteries & Tiles	2	130	495	26.26	93.59
Cotton Textiles	35	5143	59019	8.71	337.46
Jute Textiles	5	1497	19547	7.66	603.68
Silk & Woolen Textile	22	7662	51060	15.01	205.97
Paper & Paper Product	8	1240	15713	7.89	381.97
Elect. Equipment	31	5421	26344	20.58	134.71
Engineering	90	22551	147236	15.32	220.58
Chemicals	68	21504	143875	14.95	197.76
Sugar & Breweries	9	992	5861	16.93	177.96
Food Products	19	4644	15976	29.07	99.18
Plantations	40	4508	29413	15.33	204.04
Others	68	10532	68954	15.27	190.67
Total	435	98860	716796	13.80	218.42

* Equity = Cum Bonus Equity.

For example the amount of bonus issues for Banking and Insurance industry is Rs. 4.74 crores and this has been Rs. 93.47 crores for the Metals group, i.e., an increase by 18.72 times. On the other hand pre-bonus reserves between these two industry groups have increased by 55.78 times. With such variation i.e., change in pre-bonus reserves substantially outpouring the changes in bonus amounts between two industry groups being compared one may expect a decline in bonus percentage depending upon the degree or the extent by which changes in pre-bonus reserves out pours the changes in the amount of bonus. Again we can compare Metals with Electric Generation. The amount of bonus declines by 0.04 times and pre-bonus reserves by 0.08 times which again shows change in reserves out pouring the changes in the bonus amount as a result of which bonus percentage further declines and goes down from

9.39 per cent for Metals to 5.81 per cent.

The variations in bonus percentage over industry groups are indeed interesting. For example the bonus rate star performer Jute industry which always came out with 1:1 ratio has only got a very low bonus percentage at 7.66. This may mean that Jute firms have shown a greater aggressiveness in their bonus behaviour.

The bonus percentage will thus be found to be determined by the variations in the pre-bonus reserves and the amount of bonus. We have used another measure for the bonus performance of industry groups which we have called Average Bonus Ratio [vide Table - 3.8]. The latter measure relates the bonus amount to pre- bonus equity whereas the bonus percentage in Table - 3.13 relates the bonus amount to pre-bonus reserves. Since the pre-bonus reserves and the pre-bonus equity are the two independent variables entering our twin measure of bonus performance by industries one may be interested to explore the relationship between the two measures of bonus performance. This relationship is given by the following formula:

BP = [ABR x [PBE/PBR)]

where BP = Bonus percentage

ABR = Average Bonus Ratio

PBR = Pre-Bonus Reserves and

PBE = Pre-Bonus Equity capital.

From the above formula the ABR can be found out as follows

ABR = [BP x (PBR/PBE)]

VII. Summary and Findings

This Chapter was addressed to study the bonus issues made during 1977-88 with regard to the number, ratios, amount, size of bonus issues along with the size of the companies issuing bonus shares and the aggregate trends in the capitalisation of reserves. A sidelight of this study is an industry-wise analysis of bonus issues made during the study period. Following is a list of conclusions emerging from the analysis.

1. The years 1985-87 have witnessed a spurt in the number of bonus issues being made by companies especially due to the relaxations given to closely held companies.

2. A little less than half of the companies have issued bonus shares more than once during the study period and majority of the successive bonus issues have come within four years gap

3. A very important characteristic feature of the bonus issues made by the Indian corporate sector is that significant part of the bonus issues are made in certain high ratios especially in the ratios of 1:1, 1:2, 3:5, and 2:5. In addition, there is almost a sudden shift in the ratio of capitalisation during 1983-88 when compared to 1977-82. Bonus issues in the ratio of 1:1 have almost doubled during 1983-88 and ratio 1:2 has been relegated to the second position.

4. After 1985 there is a sudden and abrupt step-up in the aggregate amount of bonus issues. The years 1986-88 alone have accounted for a 49.6% of the total amount of bonus issues of the study period though the number of bonus issues are just 29.7%. Incidentally it is during this period that the market was 'unrealistically' buoyant which virtually 'lit up the heavens'

5. The orientation of the Government headed by Rajiv Gandhi was towards growth through industrialisation and the liberalisation of fiscal and economic policies seems to have given fillip to a high degree capitalisation of reserves. This is evident if we observe the average annual number of bonus issues which soared to 45 and average bonus ratio was 0.59 during 1985-88.

6. A striking point is that 28.5% of the bonus issues are of less than Rs. 50 lakhs and 48.05% are of less than Rs. 100 lakhs and this implies that a major chunk of the bonus issues during the study period are made by small and medium rather than large companies in terms of their pre-bonus equity size.

7. The corporate sector appears to be following a measured inaggressiveness in capitalisation of its reserves as is reflected by the average percentage of capitalisation of available pre- bonus reserves which works out to 14%.

8. Engineering and Chemicals lead in the number of bonus issues made during the period. Jute industry ranks first in the average bonus ratio notwithstanding its lowest rate of capitalisation of reserves.

9. Those industries which are either in public utility or under price controls tend to be less frequent in bonus issues and not liberal in capitalisation of reserves.

IV

Bonus Shares - Dividend Changes

I. Introduction

Although there has been a continuing theoretical controversy on the dividend effects on share value[1], dividend has been found to be an active variable in empirical investigations conducted in Indian capital market.In fact, the pioneering duo in the realm of security analysis has gone to the extent of suggesting that managements be required to use as much energy and foresight in order to maintain the announced dividend policy as they employ in the general conduct of the corporate affairs.[3]

The debate on the market significance of bonus shares has also underlined the valuation effects of dividends. The theoretical propositions that share values are affected by what happened to dividend policy and not just by how much and at what point of time bonus shares in a certain rate have been announced or issued. The concern of the present chapter is to further expose this debate to the empirical data relating to the Indian corporate sector.

Equity share prices are by and large a result of the market process through which net cash flows accruing to investors over their investment time horizon in the form of regular dividends and terminal gains. It has been found, however, that the investor experience over long holding periods of five years or more has been one of capital losses in general; capital gains, in fact, didn't occur as widely as is generally believed.[4] This makes regular dividends as a key variable in the share valuation process in the long run. In view of this one may naturally expect to look at the size of dividend cake after the bonus issue, so that ex-bonus dividend [both rate and quantum] will be an important parameter in all reckonings by market participants. It is not an exaggeration to state that a bonus will be meaningful in real terms only if the shareholders get a larger quantum of dividend after the bonus than what they received before. This in turn will happen when [a] dividend rate is same as the pre-bonus dividend rate; or [b] when this rate is higher than the pre-bonus rate and [c] when the dividend rate on the post-bonus capital is less than the pre-bonus capital but the reduction in the rate is less than the bonus rate. Thus, the shareholder expectations on the eve of bonus issue regarding the post-bonus dividend becomes a key determinant of the value of the equity share. It will therefore, be widely appreciated that the shareholders' belief about bonus shares bringing in an additional dividend flow or at least not cutting the absolute dividend slice is not unrealistic. This analysis makes an attempt to observe whether the pre-bonus dividend rate, as generally expected by shareholders, is maintained after bonus issue, whether the shareholder has an increased quantum of dividend as a result of bonus issues, and if so, what is the magnitude and relation to bonus rate of such receipts and whether such increases in the quantum of dividend are truly associated with bonus issues.

The number of bonus issues analysed for this purpose is 415 [refer to Table-4A]. Because of the non-availability of dividend data for three bonus issues they have been excluded from our original sample of 435. Of the remaining, four issues have a skipped dividend record in the immediately preceding year of bonus issue and 13 have skipped dividends in the bonus year. These 13 bonus issues appeared to be in lieu of dividend which the new guidelines effective from 1982 seek to prohibit. Our analysis therefore does not include these 20 bonus issues for want of associated dividend record. Table-4A provides a detailed break down of our sample companies and their bonus issues. As will be seen the number of companies has been split according to a two way matrix which provides an industry wise break down and according to frequency of bonus issues.

Section one of the present chapter has been directed to identify dividends as key variable effecting the value of share. This section also specifies and explains the sample. Section two explains the parameters evolved to measure the dividend changes. It also caries an example to illustrate the arithmetic of dividend changes and adjustment factor. Section three presents statistical evidence to show if the common belief of the shareholder that companies tend to maintain nominal dividend rate after the bonus issue has any reality or not. Section four makes an attempt to portray if bonus issues resulted in an increased flow of dividends to shareholders. Section five analyses the magnitude of increase in post-bonus dividends and also the dividend advantage derived by the shareholders consequent to bonus issue. Section six attempts to relate dividend changes to bonus issues by observing the track of pre and post-bonus dividend changes. The last section summarises the important findings emerging from the statistical analysis undertaken in this chapter.

Table -4A

Frequency of Bonus Issues — An Industry Classification

Industry	Number of Companies with the Frequency of Bonus Issues				No. of Companies	No. of Issues
	One	Two	Three	Four		
Banking & Insurance	0	2	0	0	2	4
Metals	12	5	0	0	17	22
Elect. Generation	2	0	0	0	2	2
Trading	1	0	0	0	1	1
Coal & Mining	1	0	1	0	2	4
Cement	1	1	0	0	2	3
Potteries & Tiles	2	0	0	0	2	2
Cotton Text	10	10	1	0	21	33
Jute Text	1	1	0	0	2	3
Silk & Woolen Text	7	2	2	1	12	21
Paper & Paper Products	4	2	0	0	6	8
Elec. Equip	11	5	3	0	19	30
Engineering	20	19	8	1	48	86
Chemicals	17	14	7	0	38	66
Sugar & Breweries	7	1	0	0	8	9
Food Products	2	3	3	0	8	17
Plantations	7	9	5	0	21	40
Others	22	8	6	2	38	64
Total	127	82	36	4	249	415

II. The Measurement of Dividend Changes

Nominal dividend rates have been used for the purpose of observing the dividend tracks since they permit comparison among the issues and over the period of time. To analyse the pre-bonus and post-bonus changes in the quantum of dividend the nominal dividend rates of the bonus year and all other subsequent years have been adjusted according to the bonus rates of the respective bonus issues.

To explain and derive the adjusting factor for the post- bonus dividend rates we use the following notations:

D_t = nominal dividend rate of the bonus year

D_{t-1} = nominal dividend rate of the immediately preceding year of the bonus year

B = bonus rate.

Q = pre-bonus paid up capital.

From the above notations it can be derived that:

1. Post-bonus paid up capital = Q[1+B]
2. Post-bonus dividend quantum = $QD_t[1+B]$
3. Post-bonus dividend quantum relative to pre-bonus paid up capital:

$$= [\{QD_t (1+B)\} \{Q\}^{-1}] = D_t[1+B] ...4.1$$

Simply stated the adjusted dividend rate of the bonus year and all other subsequent years is a multiple of [1+B] of the respective nominal dividend rates. The quality of bonus issue can be measured in terms of magnitude of change in the dividend quantum. The magnitude of change can be determined as follows using the above notations:

Pre-bonus dividend quantum = QD_{t-1}

Post-bonus dividend quantum = $QD_t[1+B]$

Variance between pre and post-bonus quantum of dividend

$$= [\{QD_t(1+B)\} - QD_{t-1}] .... 4.2$$

$$\text{The relative variance} = [\{D_t(1+B)\} - D_{t-1}][D_{t-1}]^{-1} .... 4.3$$

A point worth mentioning is that the magnitude of change in post-bonus dividend quantum may not necessarily be a result of bonus issue. Thus to highlight the change in the post-bonus dividend quantum as a consequence of bonus issue we hereunder make a 'component variance analysis' where we segregate the total change or variance in the post-bonus dividend quantum on the basis of factors causing such variance. They are: 1. Dividend Rate Variance; and 2. Variance in the quantum of paid-up capital. Dividend rate variance results when the post-bonus dividend rate is at variance from the pre-bonus rate. The extent to which this difference contributes to the total variance is the dividend rate variance [DRV]. This can be calculated as follows:

$$\text{Dividend Rate Variance} = [D_t - D_{t-1}]Q ....4.4$$

The increment in the paid-up capital as a consequence to bonus issue is another factor that contributes to the total variance in the quantum of dividend. This is the Capital Quantum Variance [CQV]. Notationally expressed this will be as follows:

$$\text{Capital Quantum Variance} = [\{Q(1+B)\} - \{Q\}]D_t$$

$$=QBD_t .... 4.5$$

This variance will always be positive or favourable. If the relative component variances are to be calculated they will be:

a. Relative DRV = $\{[D_t - D_{t-1}]Q\}\{QD_{t-1}\}^{-1}$....4.6

b. Relative CQV = $[QBD_t][QD_{t-1}]^{-1}$..... 4.7

It may be noted that the bonus context variance is the capital quantum variance since this is the extent to which the total dividend quantum variance occurred as a result of bonus issue. But in determining the bonus quality both the variances have a complementary role to play. This is so because the shareholder is mindful of the post-bonus aggregate dividend quantum variance which has two components as noted above. The capital quantum variance is always positive and its relative is equivalent to the post-bonus dividend rate and therefore, it is ultimately the nature and extent of rate variance that determines the quality of bonus. This is because the rate variance will be negative if $D_t < D_{t-1}$ [Equation 4.4]. The extent to which D_t can be less than D_{t-1} depends upon the allowable dilution rate. This allowable dilution rate can be easily understood if one examines the variance in the aggregate quantum of dividend with which equation 4.2 is concerned.

The equation for aggregate dividend quantum variance is:

$[(D_t\{1+B\}) - (D_{t-1})]$.... 4.2

The two independent variables that determine the variance are D_t and D_{t1} and three possible situations can be conceived. They are:

1. $D_t[1+B] < D_{t-1}$
2. $D_t[1+B] = D_{t-1}$
3. $D_t[1+B] > D_{t-1}$

In the first case the shareholder is actually at a loss in the quantum of dividend received after bonus issues and in the second case he gets the same quantum of dividend whereas in case three he really has an additional dividend inflow. These three states can be stated in other form also.

1. $D_t < [D_{t-1}\{1+B\}^{-1}]$.. Variance is Negative
2. $D_t = [D_{t-1}\{1+B\}^{-1}]$...Variance is Zero
3. $D_t > [D_{t-1}\{1+B\}^{-1}]$.. Variance is Positive

It means that if the post-bonus dividend rate is less than the bonus adjusted pre-bonus dividend rate the total quantum of post-bonus dividend decreases, if they are same there will not be any change in the quantum of pre and post-bonus dividend quantum and if post-bonus dividend rate is more than the bonus adjusted pre-bonus dividend rate the shareholder gets an additional quantum of dividend after the bonus issue. The shareholder's assessment about the quality of bonus is a function of nature and direction of change in the post-bonus dividend rate. Thus, his assessment regarding the bonus quality is negative, indifferent and positive under the three situations listed above respectively.

The point that the shareholder reacts positively to bonus issues if the post-bonus dividend rate is more than the bonus adjusted pre-bonus dividend rate is clear from the above argument. This implies that a shareholder tends to be positively disposed towards bonus issues if and only if the post-bonus dividend rate is more than the bonus adjusted pre-bonus dividend rate. The allowable extent of dilution in the pre-bonus dividend rate relative to pre-bonus dividend rate is as follows:

$[D_{t-1}-\{D_{t-1}(1+B)^{-1}\}]\,[D_{t-1}]^{-1}$..... 4.8

The relative variance of post-bonus dividend rate from bonus adjusted pre-bonus dividend rate can be measured by the following formula:

$[D_t-\{D_{t-1}(1+B)^{-1}\}][D_{t-1}]^{-1}$.... 4.9

The ratio of relative post-bonus dividend rate variance from the bonus adjusted pre-bonus dividend rate to the relative allowable extent of dilution gives us an interesting measurement of dividend advantage/ dividend elasticity.

$[[D_t-\{D_{t-1}(1+B)^{-1}\}][D_{t-1}]^{-1}][D_t-D_{t-1}\{1+B\}^{-1}]$

$[D_{t-1}]^{-1}]^{-1}$

$=[[D_t-\{D_{t-1}(1+B)^{-1}\}][D_{t-1}-\{D_{t-1}(1+B)^{-1}\}]^{-1}]$

$=[\{D_t(1+B)\}-D_{t-1}][D_{t-1}B]^{-1}$.....4.10

An example may illustrate the point more clearly

Escorts has given in 1987 a bonus in the ratio of 3:5 [bonus rate = 60%]. Pre-bonus dividend in 1986 was 22% and the same was the post-bonus dividend in 1987 too.

The magnitude of dividend change as calculated using equation 4.3 will be:

$(\{22\%[1+.60]\}\ (22\%)^{-1} = 0.60$ or 60%

The Dividend Rate Variance as per equation 4.6

$=[22\%-22\%][22\%]^{-1}$ which for all practical purposes is zero.

The Capital Quantum Variance as per equation 4.7

$=[22\%\text{x}60\%][22\%]^{-1} = 0.60$ or 60%

The dividend advantage as calculated using equation 4.10 will be:

$(\{22\%[1+.60]\} - 22\%)(22\%[0.60])^{-1} = 1.00$ or 100%

These figures speak out the facts very clearly that the post-bonus quantum of dividend has increased by 60 per cent and after bonus issue the company has maintained the dividend rate as it was before and therefore, the shareholder has been given 100 per cent of pre-bonus dividend rate even on the bonus shares. In other words, Rate of increase in dividend quantum is 60% and the shareholder has got an extra 100% of pre-bonus dividend rate on the bonus shares also.

These measures are useful in measuring the direction and extent of change in the post-bonus dividend. But, whether these changes are attributable to bonus issue alone remains to be a question unanswered so far. To be more specific if bonus issue has any specific centripetal force on dividends, remains to be analysed. For this purpose we have analysed the relative change in dividends during the five year period centering the bonus year, i.e., five years include two years each before and after and the bonus year, to avoid the temporal changes in basic conditions governing the dividends. The possible objection of non comparability of years is eased by breaking the entire study period of 12 years into three sub-periods of four years each. These three sub-periods are 1. 1977-80, 2. 1981-84 and 3. 1985-88. The significance of this breakdown as has already been mentioned in Chapter-III may be recalled that the first sub-period coincides with the pre-1981 bonus guidelines, the second sub-period is immediately followed the revision of bonus guidelines and the third sub-period is coterminous with the capital market buoyancy and also witnessed a few modifications in the guidelines. The data of dividend changes have been used to note if the changes in dividend during the bonus year have any specific association with bonus issue. We have also conducted ANOVA on growth rates in bonus adjusted dividend rates to further strengthen our observation in this regard. Growth rates have been calculated using the following formula:

$[\{D_i - D_{i-1}\}\{D_{i-1}\}^{-1}]$.... 4.11

Where D_i = dividend rate of the year

D_{i-1} = dividend rate of the preceding year

III. Post-Bonus Changes in Dividend Rates

The common belief of the shareholders is that the issue of bonus by the company is a signal of the company's intention to increase the dividend distribution in the near future. Some feel that the pre-bonus dividend rate is maintained even after the bonus issue and thus results in an increase in the quantum of dividend in the proportion of bonus ratio. It is this facet of the bonus issue that is considered to be the criteria for judging the bonus quality.

The insistence of the guidelines causing managements to announce their post-bonus dividend intentions is linked up with the objective that the exercise for determining the proposed bonus ratio is done very carefully after taking into account the cash flow implications of a bonus ratio. The market interprets this as a case of a likely increase in the post-bonus dividend quantum and calculations of a more conservative among the market men do anticipate that the company in the first place does not reduce the dividend rate and even if it does so for any pressing reasons the reduction is well within the limits of the bonus ratio. The implication is that the market is not prepared to witness a cut in the total dividend quantum after bonus without at the same time penalising the price of the share.

Our analysis is performed on three sets of data: 1. post- bonus dividend rate changes for different years over time; 2. post-bonus rate changes for different industry groups during the period of study and 3. post-bonus dividend rate changes over the period of study for different bonus sizes.

Table - 4.1

Changes in Unadjusted Dividend Rate of the Bonus Year from the Dividend Rate of Immediately Preceding Year for Bonus Issues Made During 1977-88

Year	Increase		No Change		Decrease		Total	
	No.	%	No.	%	No.	%	No.	%
1977	6	22.22	10	37.04	11	40.74	27	100
1978	7	24.14	14	48.28	8	27.59	29	100
1979	4	15.38	12	46.15	10	38.46	26	100
1980	5	14.29	11	31.43	19	54.29	35	100
1981	4	14.29	9	32.14	15	53.57	28	100
1982	5	10.64	15	31.91	27	57.45	47	100
1983	4	12.50	11	34.38	17	53.12	32	100
1984	5	21.74	5	21.74	13	56.52	23	100
1985	13	27.66	17	36.17	17	36.17	47	100
1986	7	15.91	11	25.00	26	59.09	44	100
1987	10	18.18	20	36.36	25	45.45	55	100
1988	4	18.18	8	36.36	10	45.45	22	100
Total	74	17.83	143	34.46	198	47.71	415	100

Table-4.1 tabulates the data for the period 1977-88 relating to the number of bonus issues which were accompanied by an increase, a decrease and a maintenance of the dividend rate of the pre-bonus year. During the study period of twelve years direction of change in the post-bonus nominal dividend rate from that of immediately preceding year are tabulated in Table-4.1. It can be noted from table that majority of the bonus issues followed either with an increased or an unchanged nominal dividend rate compared to the immediately preceding year. Out of the 415 bonus issues 74 [17.83%] witnessed an increase in the post-bonus nominal dividend rate and 143 [34.46%] were accompanied by a nominal dividend rate equivalent to the pre- bonus rate. Of a total number of 29 bonus issues in 1978 seven were accompanied by an increase in the nominal dividend rate and 14 issues by an unchanged dividend rate. This means that 72.41 per cent [21/28] of the bonus issues of 1978 have responded to shareholders expectations. It may be noted that the year 1978 recorded the smallest number of post-bonus dividend decreases both in absolute and relative terms. 40.91 per cent of the total bonus issues were accompanied by dividend rates that were maintained or increased dividend rate. It is interesting to note that the number of bonus issues where a dividend rate was eithermaintained or increased was less than 48 per cent during the years 1980-84. This is the period during which fresh guidelines have come into force and witnessed many modification also. From the table it can be seen that majority of the issues over the period have seen the post-bonus dividend rate equivalent to or more than the pre-bonus dividend rate and thus benefited the shareholders with additional quantum of dividend.

Table-4.2 presents industry-wise data for the number of bonus issues and the associated direction of change in the post bonus dividend rate. It will be seen that the industries which have announced 20 or more bonus issues during the period of study are metals, cotton textiles, silk and woolen textiles, electric equipment, engineering, chemicals, plantations and others. Except engineering and electric equipment in all other industry groups with 20 or more bonus issues the number of issues followed by an increase or a constancy of the post-bonus dividend rate together exceeds the number associated with a decrease in the post-bonus dividend rate. This gives the semblance of a relationship that more liberal the industry in issuing the bonus shares the more liberal it is in its post-bonus dividend rate. In the case of electric equipment and engineering, however, the number of issues with increased and constant dividend rates together is less than the number of decreased dividend rates. One is tempted to conclude from this that this non traditional industry group though liberal in issuing bonus shares has not been equally liberal either in increasing the post-bonus dividend rate or at least maintaining it. It is thus obvious that the evidence is of a mixed character and no unique pattern correlating the liberal bonus issues and liberal dividend rate for the post-bonus period emerges at the level of industry group.

Table - 4.2

Changes in Unadjusted Dividend Rate of the Bonus Year from the Dividend Rate of the Immediately Preceding Year for Bonus issues made by Different Industries During 1977-88

Industry	Increase		No Change		Decrease		Total	
	No.	%	No.	%	No.	%	No.	%
Banking & Insurance	2	50.00	2	50.00	0	0.00	4	100
Metals	5	22.73	9	40.91	8	36.36	22	100
Elec. Generation	0	0.00	2	100.00	0	0.00	2	100
Trading	1	100.00	0	0.00	0	0.00	1	100
Coal & Mining	0	0.00	2	50.00	2	50.00	4	100
Cement	1	33.33	0	0.00	2	66.67	3	100
Potteries & Tiles	1	50.00	0	0.00	1	50.00	2	100
Cotton Text	3	9.09	14	42.42	16	48.48	33	100
Jute Text	0	0.00	0	0.00	3	100.00	3	100
Silk & Woolen Text	4	19.05	12	57.14	5	23.81	21	100
Paper & Paper Products	1	12.50	2	25.00	5	62.50	8	100
Elec. Equip	7	23.33	7	23.33	16	53.33	30	100
Engineering	13	15.12	21	24.42	52	60.47	86	100
Chemicals	12	18.18	26	39.39	28	42.42	66	100
Sugar & Breweries	3	33.33	1	11.11	5	55.56	9	100
Food Products	2	11.76	6	35.29	9	52.94	17	100
Plantations	10	25.00	11	27.50	19	47.50	40	100
Others	9	14.06	28	43.75	27	42.19	64	100
Total	74		143		198		415	

Table-4.3 presents data on bonus size and the associated direction of change in the post-bonus dividend rate. The bonus percentage has been classified into 7 sizes of which the first two size groups resemble the stock splits of the US pattern. It must be mentioned that the size classification does not follow any legal basis or any accounting conventions. It will be noted that around 65.75 per cent of the total bonus issues are of a size which is equal to or less than 60 per cent. In the case of all those issues the combined number of increased and constant dividend rates during the post-bonus period exceeds the number of reduced dividend rates. The relationship witnesses a reversal in the case of bonus issues exceeding 60 per cent and to the extended rate of 100 per cent. In fact, bonus issues within the size range of 80-100 per cent appear to be a very interesting category where 80 out of 124 bonus issues have been followed by a decrease in the dividend rate. While the same is true to the size group of 60-80 per cent where 12 out of 22 bonus issues were followed by a decrease in the dividend rate, it cannot possibly be generalised that higher bonus sizes are followed by decreased dividend rates.

Table - 4.3

Changes in Unadjusted Dividend Rate of the Bonus Year from the Dividend Rate of Immediately Preceding Year for Bonus Issues of Different Rates Made During 1977-88

Bonus % [BP]	Increase		No Change		Decrease		Total	
	No.	%	No.	%	No.	%	No.	%
BP≤20	5	21.74	10	43.48	8	34.78	23	100
20<BP≤25	10	34.48	9	31.03	9	31.03	28	100
25<BP≤40	12	14.12	38	44.71	31	36.47	81	100
40<BP≤60	27	18.37	53	36.05	58	39.46	138	100
60<BP≤80	5	22.73	5	22.73	12	54.55	22	100
80<BP≤100	14	11.29	27	21.77	80	64.52	121	100
BP>100	1	50.00	1	50.00	0	0.00	2	100
Total	74		143		198		415	

IV. Post Bonus Changes in Quantum of Dividend

Though it is the dividend rate that gets immediate attention of the shareholders, what really matters is the post- bonus quantum of dividend. The shareholders are really benefited if the quantum of dividends received subsequent to bonus issue is more than the pre-bonus quantum of dividend. If the former is less than the latter the bonus issue is seen as a harbinger of bad news and if both are equal the shareholder may stand indifferent to bonus issue. Thus, what we really have to examine is the changes in post-bonus dividend quantum. To throw light on this facet of bonus implications we adjusted the post-bonus dividend rates to arrive at post-bonus dividend quantum as was discussed in an earlier part. Here also our analysis is performed on the three sets of data, i.e., 1. post-bonus dividend quantum changes over time; 2. post-bonus dividend quantum changes for different industry groups during the period of study and 3. post- bonus dividend quantum changes over the period of study for different bonus sizes.

Table-4.4 portrays the year wise data for the study period on the increase, constancy and decrease of the dividend quantum followed by bonus issues. It will be seen that in around 93 per cent of the cases there has been an increase in the dividend quantum and this high percentage has been maintained in all the years. In fact, the increase has ranged between 87.23 per cent (1982) and 97.87 per cent (1985). On the basis of this evidence it may be concluded that bonus shares have consistently been of positive value to the shareholders because they have been characterised by

Table - 4.4

Change in Adjusted Dividend Rate of the Bonus Year from the Dividend Rate of Immediately Preceding Year for Bonus Issues Made During 1977-88

Year	Increase		No Change		Decrease		Total	
	No.	%	No.	%	No.	%	No.	%
1977	26	96.30	0	0.00	1	3.70	27	100
1978	27	93.10	1	3.45	1	3.45	29	100
1979	25	96.15	0	0.00	1	3.85	26	100
1980	33	94.29	1	2.86	1	2.86	35	100
1981	25	89.29	1	3.57	2	7.14	28	100
1982	41	87.23	1	2.13	5	10.64	47	100
1983	30	93.75	0	0.00	2	6.25	32	100
1984	22	95.65	0	0.00	1	4.35	23	100
1985	46	97.87	1	2.13	0	0.00	47	100
1986	39	88.64	1	2.27	4	9.09	44	100
1987	51	92.73	1	1.82	3	5.45	55	100
1988	20	90.91	2	9.09	0	0.00	22	100
Total	385	92.77	9	2.17	21	5.06	415	100

a progressive increase in their cash flows consequential upon bonus issues. This increase in cash flows should have a favourable effect on share prices other things being same. It must also get reflected in a progressive increase in the share price index during the period of study. Another point to be observed is that majority of the companies that have decreased the post-bonus dividend rate have done so at a rate less than bonus ratio. This again has a positive cash flow implications for the shareholders and will be evaluated by the market as conducive to share price increase. This implies that the reduction in the post bonus dividend rate has been less than the bonus ratio in all such cases. A comparison of 'Decrease' columns of Table 4.1 and 4.4 bears this out. It will be noticed that while the total number of issues followed by a decrease in the dividend rate over the 12 year period is 198 [Table - 4.1] only 21 [Table - 4.4] issues report a reduction in the dividend quantum. This means that 177 out of 198 cases of bonus issues were those where the dividend rate during the post-bonus period was reduced at a percentage less than the bonus ratio as a result of which the dividend quantum did not decrease. This conclusion holds good for all the 12 years of study period.

Table - 4.5

Changes in Adjusted Dividend Rate of the Bonus Year from the Dividend Rate the Immediately Preceding Year for Bonus Issues Made by Different Industries During 1977-88

Industry	Increase		No Change		Decrease		Total	
	No.	%	No.	%	No.	%	No.	%
Banking & Insurance	4	100.00	0	0.00	0	0.00	4	100
Metals	21	95.45	0	0.00	1	4.55	22	100
Elec. Generation	2	100.00	0	0.00	0	0.00	2	100
Trading	1	100.00	0	0.00	0	0.00	1	100
Coal & Mining	4	100.00	0	0.00	0	0.00	4	100
Cement	3	100.00	0	0.00	0	0.00	3	100
Potteries & Tiles	2	100.00	0	0.00	0	0.00	2	100
Cotton Text	31	93.94	0	0.00	2	6.06	33	100
Jute Text	3	100.00	0	0.00	0	0.00	3	100
Silk & Woolen Text	20	95.24	0	0.00	1	4.76	21	100
Paper & Paper Products	7	87.50	1	12.50	0	0.00	8	100
Elec. Equip	27	90.00	0	0.00	3	10.00	30	100
Engineering	82	95.35	3	3.49	1	1.16	86	100
Chemicls	61	92.42	0	0.00	5	7.58	66	100
Sugar & Breweries	8	88.89	0	0.00	1	11.11	9	100
Food Products	16	94.12	1	5.88	0	0.00	17	100
Plantations	33	82.50	3	7.50	4	10.00	40	100
Others	60	93.75	1	1.56	3	4.69	64	100
Total	385		9		21		415	

A very interesting phenomenon that can be observed in Table-4.5 which presents the industry-wise analysis of post-bonus quantum changes is that the bonus issues by industry groups which are not liberal in bonus issues during the study period appear to be intended to award the shareholders an increased dividend. So is the case with four bonus issues by two firms in Banking and Insurance group and the other groups like Electric Generation[2], Trading [1], Coal and Mining [2], Cement [2], Potteries and Tiles [2] and Jute textiles [2] follow the sert. Of the 40 bonus issues made by the 21 firms in Plantation industry 33 issues [82.5%] have an increased post-bonus dividend quantum. The performance of engineering industry emerges as relatively outstanding. Out of 86 bonus issues considered it was only one issue that followed with a decreased quantum of dividend. If we compare this figure with that in Table-4.2 it is obvious that this is the industry which liberally issued bonus shares and not maintained the pre-bonus dividend rate after bonus issue in a large number of cases but the decrease in the post-bonus dividend rate in overwheling majority of the cases has been less than the bonus rate. Therefore, the shareholders of this group of firms have always had an increment in their post-bonus quantum of dividend.

Table-4.6 presents the data on the direction of change in the dividend quantum related to various bonus sizes. It will be seen that the bonus size range 40-60 and 80-100 are the most favoured groups as a whole and for all the years of the study period. In a vast majority of the cases within these most favoured groups, the dividend quantum showed an increase. While the increase in the dividend quantum accompanies an equally large number of cases for other size goups, it is relatively low for the smallest bonus size class. But this is a very unusual and a typical case and therefore does not affect the broad conclusion reached in the case of the most favoured size groups.

Table-4.6

Changes in Bonus Adjusted Dividend Rate of the Bonus Year from the Dividend Rate of Immediately Preceding Year for Bonus Issues of Different Rates Made During 1977-88

Bonus Percentage	Increase		No Change		Decrease		Total	
	No.	%	No.	%	No.	%	No.	%
BP≤20	18	78.26	0	0.00	5	21.74	23	100
20<BP≤25	27	96.43	1	3.57	0	0.00	28	100
25<BP≤40	72	88.89	0	0.00	9	11.11	81	100
40<BP≤60	131	94.93	2	1.45	5	3.62	138	100
60<BP≤80	22	100.00	0	0.00	0	0.00	22	100
80<BP≤100	113	93.39	6	4.96	2	1.65	121	100
BP>100	2	100.00	0	0.00	0	0.00	2	100
Total	385		9		21		415	

V. Extent of Dividend Quantum Changes

It has been observed that an overwhelming majority of the bonus issues brought with them increased cash dividends to the shareholders. What is rather more important is not the nature or direction of dividend changes but the extent of change. In this section therefore, we bring together data relating to the changes and magnitude in the dividend and bonus sizes. It has been arranged in the form of a two way matrix in Table-4.7. Altogether nine classes of dividend increase and six classes of bonus sizes have been tabulated in 54 cells [9x6]. For each bonus size there are four rows. First row provides a count of the number of cases, second row provides the percentage of such cases to total [385], the third row presents the percentage of such cases to row totals and the fourth row provides the percentage of these cases to column totals.

Table-4.8 is again in a two way matrix form and it presents the six bonus size classes in relation to the five elasticity of dividend rate. As in Table-4.7, for each bonus class there are four rows with the same meaning for each row.

It will be noted that Table-4.7 reveals an interesting relationship between bonus size and the size of increase in the dividend quantum. Each bonus size records the largest number of cases which at the same time belong to an identical dividend increase size. For example for the bonus size group of less than 20 per cent the largest number of cases fall in 20-30 percentage dividend increase size, for 25-40 bonus size the largest number of cases belong to 30-40 percentage cell, for 40-50 bonus dividend increase class, for the 50-60 bonus size the largest number of cases belong to 50-60 dividend percentage increase group and so on. This suggests that as bonus size increases predominant number of bonus issues will be associated with an increase in the dividend quantum of the same percentage range of the bonus size. In other words, in a vast majority of the cases the bonus size will be influencing the percentage increase in the dividend quantum also.

It can be seen from the Table-4.8 that only 21 out of 415 recorded a negative elasticity of dividend rate and this was almost equally distributed over the different bonus size classes. The largest number of cases with positive elasticity were in the 100-150 per cent group, this number being 169. As many as 114 cases had a low positive elasticity with the 0-50 per cent range. It may be recalled that the elasticity of dividend rate is a function of change in dividend quantum in the bonus year compared to the year before and the dividend quantum the year before multiplied by the bonus ratio. In view of the many different ways in which these parameters could influence the dividend rate elasticity that a clear cut relationship between bonus size and the elasticity is not coming up. Nevertheless, it is interesting to observe that the largest number of cases for all bonus sizes [excepting the highest bonus size class] fall in the 100-150 percentage elasticity class. It may be argued that in all these cases the dividend rate was either maintained or at best reduced by a proportion which was less than bonus rate. The bonus size equal to or more than 100 per cent appears to be a distinct group. The largest number of cases here fall in the low elasticity group of 0-50 per cent suggesting that in most of these cases the dividend rate was not increased but even decreased, though in a per cent less than the bonus rate. An equally large number of cases in this bonus size group fall in the typical elasticity class identified for other size groups i.e., 100-150 per cent. These must be the cases where the dividend rate was possibly increased or maintained.

Table-4.7

Bonus Size and the Magnitude of Dividend Quantum Change (Cell format: count/percent: total/percent:row/percent:col)

	Increase in Dividend Quantum [%]									
Bonus size [%]	<10	10-20	20-30	30-40	40-50	50-60	60-70	70-100	>100	Total
<25	3	0	12	0	1	0	1	0	1	18
	.78	.00	3.12	.00	.26	.00	.26	.00	.26	4.68
	16.67	.00	66.67	.00	5.56	.00	5.56	.00	5.56	
	12.50	.00	17.65	.00	3.13	.00	2.86	.00	1.85	
25-40	8	7	11	26	3	4	2	3	0	64
	2.08	1.82	2.86	6.75	.78	1.04	.52	.78	.00	16.62
	12.50	10.94	17.19	40.63	4.69	6.25	3.13	4.69	.00	
	33.33	21.21	16.18	47.27	9.38	7.84	5.71	9.09	.00	
40-50	1	5	5	1	19	3	0	2	0	36
	.26	1.30	1.30	.26	4.94	.78	.00	.52	.00	9.35
	2.78	13.89	13.89	2.78	52.78	8.33	.00	5.56	.00	
	4.17	5.15	7.35	1.82	59.38	5.88	.00	6.06		
50-60	3	8	13	10	0	35	3	12	1	85
	.78	2.08	3.38	2.60	.00	9.09	.78	3.12	.26	22.08
	3.53	9.41	15.29	11.76	.00	41.18	3.53	14.12	1.18	
	12.50	24.24	19.12	18.18	.00	68.63	8.57	36.36	1.85	
60-100	6	4	8	5	4	2	19	10	9	67
	1.56	1.04	2.08	1.30	1.04	.52	4.94	2.60	2.34	17.40
	8.96	5.97	11.94	7.46	5.97	2.99	28.36	14.93	13.43	
	25.00	12.12	11.76	9.09	12.50	3.92	54.29	30.30	16.67	
>100	3	9	19	13	5	7	10	6	43	115
	.78	2.34	4.94	3.38	1.30	1.82	2.60	1.56	11.17	29.87
	2.61	7.83	16.52	11.30	4.35	6.09	8.70	5.22	37.39	
	12.50	27.27	17.94	23.64	15.63	13.73	28.57	18.18	79.63	
Total	24	33	68	55	32	51	35	33	54	385
	6.23	8.57	17.66	14.29	8.31	13.25	9.09	8.57	14.03	100.00

Table-4.8

Bonus Size and Elaticity of Dividend Rate (Cell formal: count/percent: total/percent: row/ percent:col]

Bonus Size [%]	Elasticity in %					
	<0	0-50	50-100	100-150	>150	Total
<25	5	3	0	12	3	23
	1.20	.72	.00	2.89	.72	5.54
	21.74	13.04	.00	52.17	13.04	
	23.81	2.63	.00	7.10	6.25	
25-40	5	13	6	34	12	70
	1.20	3.13	1.45	8.19	2.89	16.87
	7.14	18.57	8.57	48.57	17.14	
	23.81	11.40	9.52	20.12	25.00	
40-50	4	6	6	22	2	40
	.96	1.45	1.45	5.30	.48	9.64
	10.00	15.00	15.00	55.00	5.00	
	19.05	5.26	9.52	13.02	4.17	
50-60	4	18	18	38	13	91
	.96	4.34	4.34	9.16	3.13	21.93
	4.40	19.78	19.78	41.76	14.29	
	19.05	15.79	28.57	22.49	27.08	
60-100	1	19	10	29	9	68
	.24	4.58	2.41	6.99	2.17	29.39
	1.47	27.94	14.71	42.65	13.24	
	4.76	16.67	15.87	17.16	18.75	
>100	2	55	23	34	9	123
	.48	13.25	5.54	8.19	2.17	29.64
	1.63	44.72	18.70	27.64	7.32	
	9.52	48.25	36.51	20.12	18.75	
Total	21	114	63	169	48	415
	5.06	27.47	15.18	40.72	11.57	100.00

VI. Pre and Post-Bonus Tracks of Dividend Quantum Changes

Since our sample shows that an overwhelming majority of bonus issues have followed with an increase in the dividend quantum a further question requiring attention is that if this increase in the quantum of dividends has any causal relationship with bonus issues. If the changes in the dividend quantum are attributable to the issue of bonus shares then the latter can be construed as a signal for a possible hike in the dividend quantum to the shareholders in the bonus year and also as indicative of the prospective posterity of the company.

We propose to analyse this association using the dividend quantum data over a period of five years centering the bonus year, i.e., dividend quantum data for the bonus year and for two years on either side of the bonus year. The companies that have a skipped dividend record in any one of the five year period and those for which dividend information is incomplete have been excluded since they make analysis ambiguous. This criterion has reduced our sample size to 309 bonus issues. With this five year data we could observe the change in dividend quantum for four years, the first year being the base year and hence gets eliminated. Thus, we have recorded the dividend changes for one year before bonus year [Y_{t-1}], bonus year [Y_t], one year after bonus year [Y_{t+1}], and two years after bonus year [Y_{t+2}]. The cases where the dividend quantum has increased have been worked as percentage of total cases and this figure has been used to underline the causal relation between such increment and bonus issues for the whole period and sub-periods. We have further strengthened our observations by performing a one-way ANOVA on growth rates in dividends.

Table-4.9

Percentage of Cases with Increase in Dividend Quantum

Period	No. of Cases	Years			
		Y_{t-1}	Y_t	Y_{t+1}	Y_{t+2}
1977-80	111	23.42	94.59	48.65	36.04
1981-84	112	35.71	92.86	48.21	44.64
1985-88	86	53.49	95.35	40.70	47.67
Total	309	36.25	94.17	46.28	42.39

*Y_t = Bonus year

Table - 4.9 presents the data relating to the bonus issues accompanied by an increased quantum of dividend in the bonus year, a year before and in the two immediately following years. Bonus issues with increased dividend amount have been shown as percentages of total bonus issues for each of the sub-periods, viz., 1977-80, 1981-84 and 1985-88. For example, the figure 94.59 below year Y_t and against sub-period 1977-80 reflects the proportion of total bonus issues during the period 1977-80 accompanied by an increased dividend quantum in the bonus year itself. It is obvious from the table that the percentage of cases recording an increase is substantially high in bonus year for all the sub-periods, implying that companies generally aim at increasing aggregate dividends to the shareholders and the fact is built into their bonus decisions. This might further imply the reluctance of companies to reduce the aggregate dividend quantum as a compensatory factor for bonus. The table further reveals that the percentage of bonus cases accompanied by increased dividend quantum has been more in the two years following the bonus year compared to the year preceding the bonus year. For the two sub-periods 1977-80 and 1981-84, however, the percentages in the two following years show a decline, The position for third sub-period [1985-88] is in contrast with the first two sub-periods. In this case the post-bonus percentages are less than the pre-bonus percentages and also this shows an increasing tendency over the two years following the bonus year. Thus, both for Y_{t+1} and Y_{t+2} the percentages are 40.70 and 47.67 respectively and it will be seen that these percentages are less than the pre-bonus percentage of 53.49. It may be noted that the number of cases in the third sub-period has been the lowest of all sub-periods and the first two years of these sub-periods witnessed a boom in the capital market. Most of the issues with increased dividend quantum appeared to have been timed during this boom years of sub-periods.

The association of dividend quantum increment with the bonus issue can be further substantiated if the pre and post-bonus growth rates in dividends are analysed. Since growth rates represent both the size and direction of change they assume a more explanatory role in this context. Growth rates have been calculated using equation 4.11. We get four sets of growth rates for five years, i.e., for all years excepting the first year and notated as G1, G2, G3, and G4. G2 represents the growth rate in dividend quantum of the bonus year. These are calculated as follows:

$$G1 = [(D_{t-1} - D_{t-2})(D_{t-2})^{-1}]$$

$$G2 = [(D_{t} - D_{t-1})(D_{t-1})^{-1}]$$

$$G3 = [(D_{t+1} - D_{t})(D_{t})^{-1}]$$

$$G4 = [(D_{t+2} - D_{t+1})(D_{t+1})^{-1}]$$

Where 'D' represents the quantum of dividend and subscript the year. Thus growth rates are the relative first differences.

An examination of Part-A of Table-4.10 which presents the descriptive statistics reveals that the mean growth rate of bonus year is substantially different from other growth rates [almost six times more than the nearest mean, i.e. G3] and coefficient of variation is 2.82 times less than the nearest one, i.e. G1. This signifies that the bonus effect on the dividend quantum is significant during the bonus year.

Part-B of the table gives the result of one way ANOVA for all the growth rates. The 'F' ratio is highly significant and hence the null hypothesis that all the groups have come from same population or all groups share common characteristics cannot be accepted. Part-C of the table consists of one way ANOVA result for G1, G3, and G4 all but the bonus year growth rate.. Here the 'F' ratio is not significant, being very much less than the critical value, and hence, the null hypothesis cannot be rejected. Thus, it is the bonus year whose growth rates are vitiating the result that the null hypothesis could not be accepted.

Table-4.10

Growth Rates in Dividend Quantum

Part-A: Descriptive Statistics of Growth Rates

No.	Name	N	Mean	Std. Dev.	Coefficient of Variation
1	G1	309	7.8224	23.4006	2.99
2	G2	309	48.0199	51.0670	1.06
3	G3	309	7.9381	25.8240	3.25
4	G4	309	6.3660	22.1751	4.48

Part-B: One Way ANOVA for All Growth Rates

Source	Sum of Squares	D.F.	Mean Square	F Ratio	Critical* Value
Between	383318.447	3	127772.816	118.471	
Within	1328726.241	1232	1078.512		3.78
Total	1712044.687	1235			

Part-C: One Way ANOVA for G1, G3, G4

Source	Sum of Squares	D.F.	Mean Square	F Ratio	Critical* Value
Between	474.402	2	237.201	2.398	
Within	525510.577	924	568.734		4.61
Total	525984.979	926			

* Critical Value at a significance level of 0.01

Therefore, it can be affirmed that the dividend quantum of the bonus year appears to have an association with the bonus issues since the sample size, industry composition and time coverage would even out the effects of random factors on the outcome.

VII. Summary and Findings

It has been an empirically tested conclusion that it is primarily the dividends that play a vital role in determining the equity value in the context of Indian environment. Equally emphatic are the conclusions of research studies that bonus shares *'pre se'* have no value but for the attendant dividend changes. Therefore, it has been our attempt in this chapter to analyse the post-bonus dividend changes. In this we examined the nature and extent of changes in the post-bonus dividend rate and quantum and also attempted to test if there is any 'associative' role of bonus in these changes.

The number of bonus issues included in this analysis is 415 and to ascertain the association of dividend change with the bonus issue we have observed the dividend tracks of 309 issues since they have a non-skipped dividend record during the five year period centering the bonus year. To analyse the extent of change in dividends we used magnitude of change as well as the elasticity of dividend rate. To highlight the associative role of bonus issue in dividend change we have banked on ANOVA. The findings emerging from the analysis may be summarised as below:

1. Majority of the companies with bonus issues during the study period have either maintained or increased the post-bonus dividend rate and thus appeared to have used it as a decision signaling an increment in the dividend quantum.

2. An industry-wise analysis of post-bonus dividend changes shows an inverse relationship between the frequency of bonus issues and dividend rate increase. Another related finding is that those bonus issues of the industries which are not liberal, if not aggressive, in bonus issues appeared to be clearly meant for increasing the post-bonus dividend quantum.

3. An analysis of dividend rate changes according to bonus size suggests that a lower bonus ratio will be associated with a greater possibility of dividend rate being maintained or even increased. Also, the higher the bonus ratio higher are the chances of maintaining the dividend rate in the post-bonus period especially for a bonus rate of above 25 per cent. This observation is further strengthened by our dividend quantum analysis for various bonus rates. This analysis has brought out a clear positive association between the bonus size and chances of improved post-bonus dividend quantum. Bonus issues of lower rates appeared to have a sort of complementary role to dividend and not the one of increasing it.

4. The magnitude of increase in the dividend quantum is almost always in proportion to the bonus rate. The companies have a tendency to pass on a benefit of increased dividend quantum to the shareholders but often within the range of bonus rate.

5. An overwhelming majority of bonus issues witnessed an increased post-bonus dividend quantum. In addition it is also observed

that bonus issues had a spill over effect in the sense that the percentage of cases with improved dividend quantum in the two following years is more than the preceding year. This association of bonus issue with increase in the dividend quantum became more pronounced through our ANOVA exercise. The ANOVA result for the growth rate groups of the preceding year and the two following years could not refute the null hypothesis that the groups are similar in means at 0.01 significance level whereas ANOVA result for growth rate groups including the bonus year growth rate could not accept the null hypothesis. Thus, we are unable to conclude that there is no association between the bonus issue and the growth rate of dividend quantum in bonus year.

It can, therefore, be concluded that bonus issues lead to an increased dividend quantum and an empirical association between the two has been clearly underlined by our analysis. It may be inferred that a bonus issue has an informational content with regard to future dividend quantum though not always. The issue of bonus, thus, can be construed as a signal for the prospective posterity of the company.

References

1a. Modigliani, F., and Miller H.M., The Cost of Capital, Corporation Finance, and the Theory of Investment, American Economic Review, Vol. 48, (July 1958), pp. 261-297

1b. Gordon, M.J., The Investment, Financing and Valuation of the corporation, Homewood, III. Richard. D Irwin Inc., 1962.

1c. Walter, J.E., Dividend Policies and Common Stock Prices, The Journal of Finance, Vol. XI, (March 1956), pp. 29-41.

2a. Prasanna Chandra: Valuation of Equity Shares in India, Sultan Chand & Sons, New Delhi, pp. 10.

2b. Khurana, P.K., Dividend Policies In India, Panchsheel Publications, New Delhi, 1985.

3. Benjamin Graham, David Dodd: Security Analysis-Principles and Technique, McGraw Hill Book Company Inc., 1951, pp. 589.

4. Gupta, L.C.: Rates of Return on Equity: The Indian Experience, Oxford University Press, 1981, pp. 67.

V

Valuation Effects of Bonus Shares

I. Introduction

It has been noted in Chapter-I that empirical studies both suggesting and refuting the existence of a relation between bonus share issues and prices are available. Most of these studies have derived their conclusions through an approach of elimination or exclusion of the impact of changes in variables regarded by some as 'other variables' and by others as 'more fundamental variables'. No one, thus, has included bonus issue as a determinant of the underlying changes in the share price. Most of these studies, in other words, have not attempted to identify, incorporate and observe the issue of bonus shares as an independent variable in a comprehensive share valuation model. This chapter attempts to catalyse this gap by introducing the bonus share variable along with the total time span over which it is likely to initiate and create an impact on the market. As will be noted in the later sections we extend this time span within a range of 90 days before announcement and 365 days after the announcement.

We can explain the structure of the chapter as follows: Section one provides a brief introduction to the thrust we intend to provide to the problem of relationship between the bonus shares and share valuation. Section two contains the details of the sample used for this chapter and the section that follows describes the methodology employed in the analysis. Section four contains the analysis of price relatives to highlight the possible bonus issue implications for equity share prices. Section five tests the statistical significance of issue of bonus shares as an independent variable along with the 'others' that are likely to influence share prices. The last section contains a brief outline of the findings of this chapter.

II. The Sample

We have included 121 bonus issues made by 79 companies during 1979-88 in this analysis. In fact, we gathered information for 196 bonus issues. It may be noted that the Bombay Stock Exchange Sensitive Index [BSESI] is one of the independent variables of our equation reflecting the market variations over time. Since 45 of the 196 bonus issues were announced prior to July 1, 1979 and BSESI could be made available only after that, these 45 issues have been excluded from our study. Of the remaining 151 issues, 20 have been dropped due to non-listing of the concerned shares on the Bombay Stock Exchange [BSE] as on the announcement date and another 10 have been excluded on account of non-frequent trading of the share. Table-5.1 presents the sample details regarding the year, bonus size and number. It also contains the number of companies and the frequency of their bonus issues.

As will be seen from Table-5.1 we are including 121 bonus issues made by 79 companies. This sample covers one issue each of 45 companies, two each of 26 companies and three issues each of 8 companies made during the period 1979-88. A year-wise and bonus size-wise break down of these issues has also been shown in Table-5.1. It can be seen in the table that 58 issues were in the size group of less than or equal to 50% and there are as many as 63 in the size group exceeding 50%. It will be further mentioned that the bonus issues do not show any time pattern for either of the two size groups.

Table-5.1

Details of the Sample for Analysing the Price Implications

No. of Issues	No. of Companies	Total No. of Issues
1	45	45
2	26	52
3	8	24
Total	79	121

Year	Bonus Rate in Percentage		Total
	<50%	<50%	
1979	1	1	2
1980	5	3	8
1981	6	2	8
1982	6	7	13
1983	3	7	10
1984	3	6	9
1985	11	5	16
1986	5	12	17
1987	12	9	21
1988	6	11	17
Total	58	63	121

III. Methodology

As has been mentioned and discussed in Chapter-I we compiled the closing price data as on the following dates:

a. 90 days before the announcement date [t-90]

b. 30 days before the announcement date [t-30]

c. 15 days before the announcement date [t-15]

d. Announcement date [t]

e. 15 days after the announcement date [t+15]

f. 30 days after the announcement date [t+30]

g. 90 days after the announcement date [t+90]

h. 180 days after the announcement date [t+180]

i. 270 days after the announcement date [t+270]

j. 365 days after the announcement date [t+365]

It may also be recalled that the closing price quoted immediately preceding the specified date has been used in the event of the specified date being a non-trading day for the BSE or in the event of the scrip not being traded on that date. The cum-bonus rates generally became ex-bonus after 180 days. We have extended our period of study for this purpose beyond 180 days. The timings are 270 days [t+270] and 365 days [t+365] after the announcement date. It may be noted that the price data for the period t+90 to t+365 is a mix of cum-bonus and ex-bonus quotations. Ex-bonus price quotations were few begining with the time point t+90, they were recorded for a majority of cases at the time point t+80 and in all cases for the remaining two time points, viz., t+270 and t+365. The disparity in the price data has been removed by adjusting all ex-bonus quotations for bonus and transforming them into cum-bonus prices. Thus, our analysis has been based for the entire time range on a consistent set of cum-bonus prices.

Our analysis covers two approaches outlined in an earlier part of this chapter, viz., 'excluding the implications of other variables', and 'bonus as an independent variable in the market valuation process'. In section four we cover the former approach and analyse the price relatives calculated on the basis of 'exclusion method'. Section five consists of the analysis of bonus as an independent price determining variable. The fifth section, again has two approaches; 1. bonus as presented by dummy variable and 2. test of coincidence. The details of these approaches are discussed in the forth coming section.

Price relatives for various time points are calculated with the price and the BSESI at t-90 as base. This has been done on the assumption that t-90 is the earliest conceivable time point when the market will not have been the remotest of rumour about the possible bonus [the clean time base]. The price relative calculation has been done through the following formula:

$$PR_{ij} = [(P_{ij})(P_{it-90})^{-1}][(S_j)(S_{t-90})^{-1}]^{-1}$$

Where PR_{ij} = Price Relative of share 'i' as at a time point of 'j'

P_{ij} = Closing price of share 'i' as at a time point of 'j'

P_{it-90} = Base date price of share 'i'

S_j = BSESI as at the time point 'j'

S_{t-90} = BSESI as on base date

The price relatives thus calculated represent share prices excluding the effects of general market movement. Since bonus issues in the sample do not have any other company specific simultaneous announcement, analysis of the price relatives will bring forth the bonus specific price changes. The focus of section four is on this analysis of the price relatives.

Section five in this chapter tests the statistical significance of bonus issue as an independent variable in the share valuation process. Though it may not be possible to identify and measure all the variables that may possibly influence the equity share prices, empirical studies have attempted to delineate some of these variables[1]. Such studies have been concerned with explaining the variations in share prices or price earnings rates or earnings price ratios using these variables in the process. It may be observed that the following variables have been used in many of these studies: 1. dividend or dividend pay out ratio, 2. retained earnings, 3. growth, 4. risk, 5. leverage and 6. size. Of the six variables, leverage appears to be a widely contended parameter influencing the value of the firm[2]. In view of this we have omitted this controversial variable from our study where focus in any case does not happen to be to evolve or test an inclusion model for the valuation of the firm. Our objective is limited to comprehend the effect of bonus variable along with 'other' variables whose effects have not been the subject matter of independent debate. We have added a surrogate for reflecting the market movements by including the BSESI so that our analysis at least in part includes the Capital Assets Pricing model[3]. It is presumed that this variable emerges from the market discounting process applied to the market returns. Our model, thus comprises the following variables:

1. Dividend Per Share
2. Growth
3. Risk

4. Size and
5. Market.

Since the bonus announcement is a qualitative variable, it is represented by a *zero-one dummy variable* in the model. A *zero* is used when the bonus issue has no influence on price and *one* is used when a bonus issue has an influence. Since we have by definition assumed a zero effect at the time point t-90 all bonus observations will be assigned a *zero*. In all other time points bouns observations are assigned a value *one*.

The specification of various time points in our study follows a broad identification of the 'market mould' both before and after announcement date of the bonus. On the basis of observations of the price making process we have reached the following impressions: 1. rumours about bonus start floating in the market before the announcement date; they show evidence of a positive pressure 15 days before announcement, a limited pressure 30 days before and a zero pressure 90 days before announcement; 2. the announcement date resolves a large part of the uncertainty about the bonus and hence the rumour element is totally scotched on this day, nevertheless, many legal formalities including the official sanction of bonus recommendation remain to materialise; 3. the period following the announcement date is observed by the market by closely monitoring the legal steps involved in getting the bonus through all firm-level and government-level steps; this period shapes gradually and effects the pricing process in a similar manner. To be able to focus attention on this total price formation process we identified t+15, t+30, t+90, t+180, t+270, and t+365 as the relevant time points when the real bonus effect starts building up and getting finally dissipated. We assumed that at t+365 the bonus effect will have been completely absorbed by the market, though in some cases this would have happened at time point t+80 or a bit earlier too. The objective of our empirical investigation is to assess the nature and extent of bonus share implication at different stages of issue [rumours, announcement and correction in price for bonus shares].

With six independent variables including the dummy variable and a dependent variable [non-dummy variable] the type of relationship we are formulating will be a multiple regression analysis. Multi-regression analysis is the most appropriate statistical technique to assess the individual and combined effect of a set of independent variables on a dependent variable and therefore, is employed in this study. To mitigate the problem of heteroscedasticity- a non-constant variance in the disturbance variable- and to postulate a multiplicative relation among the non-logarithmic variables, we preferred a log-linear model rather than a 'ratio' model. We, therefore, employ the following log linear multiple regression model.

$\log P = \log \beta_0 + \beta_1 \log D + \beta_2 \log(1+br) + \beta_3^{*} \log(1+\{\sigma/A\}) + \beta_4 \log S + \beta_5 \log M$

where P = Closing share price on a specified date

β_0 = Regression constant

D = Dividend Per Share [DPS] in the year in which bonus shares were also entitled for dividend

br = Growth rate

σ/A = Earning Instability Index

S = Size of the company

M = Market Index

β_3 *= Negative coefficient of Risk

The variables of our log-linear model are explained below:

1. The dependent variable denoted as 'P' is the closing share price as on a specified date. If that date is a non-trading day for BSE or the scrip was not traded on the day, the closing price of the scrip available immediately preceding that date is used. Only non-spot delivery, cum-dividend, cum-rights prices are considered. This procedure ensures comparability of all prices and eliminates the effects of special events like dividends and rights etc. Ex-bonus prices are converted into cum-bonus prices on the basis of the bonus ratio.

2. The independent variable denoted by 'D' stands for DPS paid during the year in which bonus shares have also been entitled for dividend. By including DPS and not EPS as an independent variable influencing the share price we have followed the well known procedure emerging from the works of Walter, Gorden and others.[4] In addition, investors are more mindful of dividend received than the earnings of the company and dividend series is more stable than the earnings series of any company.

3. The independent variable '1+br' is related to the average growth rate. This is calculated as follows:

$\{[Y_t - D_t][1+b]\} \{W_{t-1}\}^{-1}$

where Y_t = Earnings Per Share [EPS] in bonus year

D_t = DPS in bonus year

W_{t-1} = Book Value Per share in the year preceding the bonus year.

B = Bonus rate

It will be noted that growth rate is based on retained earnings which reflect internally induced pure growth of a firm and the effects of leverage need not influence it. These considerations have encouraged us to adopt the retentions based growth parameter for our model. Since retained earnings are a major source for financing net investment and also a very potential base for long run growth we opted for this measure. '$Y_t - D_t$' represents the retained earnings per share in the bonus year which needs a correction for bonus factor since W_{t-1} is related to the preceding year. Therefore, retained earnings per share of the bonus year are adjusted with [1+B] factor.

4. The independent variable $[1+(\sigma/A)]$ has been recognised as Earnings Instability Index. Here σ stands for deviation in EPS and 'A' for Assets Per Share is calculated as follows:

$$\sigma = [Y^*_t - Y_t(1+B)]$$

Where Y^*_t = Expected EPS in bonus year at the end of year 't-1' and

$Y_t(1+B)$ = Actual EPS in bonus year.

The expected EPS in bonus year i.e., Y^*_t, is arrived as follows:

$$Y^*_t = Y_{t-1}(1+br_{t-1})$$

Therefore, the expected EPS in bonus year is the present EPS times the average growth rate. The difference between the actual and expected $[Y^*_t - Y_t(1+B)]$ is the deviation $[\sigma]$ in EPS. An approximationof the instability of the leverage free rate of return is:

$$[Y^*_t - Y_t(1+B)]\,[A_t]^{-1}$$

5. The independent variable 'S' represents the size of the company in the bonus year and defined as capital employed in bonus year [Total Assets - Current Liabilities].

6. The independent variable 'M' is the Market Index. The BSESI [1978-79=100] compiled from a portfolio consisting of shares of 30 companies from both 'specified' and 'non-specified' groups. The shares which comprise the portfolio for determining the market index have been selected on the basis of market activity with due representation to the major industries. The price of each constituent of the index is weighted by the number of shares outstanding so that it will influence the index in proportion to its respective market importance. Thus, this index duly absorbs the changes in shares outstanding as a result of consolidations, fresh issues, rights issue, or bonus issue. Since our sample consists of those companies whose shares are frequently traded, if not actively, and all bonus issues of companies whose shares are in the 'specified' list, it is thought

appropriate to regard this index as representative of the market movements. The BSESI corresponding to that date on which price of a share is considered is included.

As discussed above a log linear multiple regression valuation model is used firstly to test whether bonus issue has any significant beneficial or detrimental effect on market price and secondly to determine whether stocks are valued in a different manner after bonus issue or on the eve of it. A *zero - one dummy* variable was added to the valuation model to measure the effect of bonus issue. It has been pointed out that investors attach some psychological value to the bonus issue and it is said to be the reason for erratic fluctuations in the prices around the announcement date. Also many have advocated the bonus issue as a mere 'cosmetic event'. To isolate the disturbance contribued by this 'cosmetic event' with 'psychological value' to the total disturbance [residual] and to measure and highlight its effect as one of the variable participating in the process of price formation we preferred the use of dummy variable. As already mentioned a value of zero is assigned to bonus issue variable for the sets of observations of the base date [90 days before the announcement] and a value of one assigned to all the other sets of observations. The base date variables are then pooled with all other sets of observations and the regression equations estimated. This helped us to analyse the possible effect of bonus issue at different points of time.

A test of coincidence is performed to analyse if the shares are valued in a different manner after the bonus issue. To accomplish this task a regression equation for observations at different time points including the base date and for observations of various time points combined [pooled] with base date observations are determined. These two equations are then used to see if they are 'coincident'. If these two equations lie on the same hyper-plane and would, therefore, give the same value for the dependent variable, given a certain set of values for independent variables, then they are 'coincident'. If the equations are coincident then it can be inferred that the manner of post-bonus equity share valuation is not different from pre- bonus, If, however, the equations did not give the same value for the dependent variable, it can be concluded that bonus issue has an effect on the market and the equations are not coincident.

If the equations are coincident then the error sum of squares for the combined observations should be equal to the error sums of squares for the unpooled equations. The difference between the error sums of squares, thus, become the measure of the degree of coincidence or test of equality of estimators.[5] If we let 'Σe^2_p' designate the error sum of squares for the pooled observations and 'Σe^2_b' and 'Σe^2_o' to signify the error sum of squares for the unpooled base date and other observations respectively, then it can be shown that $[\Sigma e^2_p - (\Sigma e^2_b + \Sigma e^2_o)][\sigma]^{-1}$ and $[\Sigma e^2_b + \Sigma e^2_o][\sigma]^{-1}$ will have independent x^2 distributions with '$v+1$' and 'n_b+n_o-2v-2' degrees of freedom respectively. The null hypothesis that there is no difference can be verified by an 'F' distribution test and where:

$$F = [\{\Sigma e^2_p - (\Sigma e^2_b + \Sigma e^2_o)\}\{v+1\}^{-1}][\{\Sigma e^2_b + \Sigma e^2_o\}\{n_b+n_o-2v-2\}^{-1}]^{-1}$$

Where v = Number of independent variables

n_b & n_o = Number of observations in base date sampleand the one pooled with base date sample respectively.

Thus, if the observed 'F' is less than the theoretical 'F' the null hypothesis cannot be refuted and *vice versa.*

IV. Analysis of Price Relatives

It may be recalled that our hypothesis was that bonus shares will not generally increase the value of shares in the market unless followed by an increase in the cash quantum of dividend. This can be tested in different ways, ANOVA on price relatives at different time points being one such methodology. Our expectation will be that if bonus issue has no implication on the value of the firm the means of different observation must be equal and *vice verse.* To test null hypothesis that all samples have come from the same population we performed the 'ANOVA' whose result along with descriptive statistics are presented in Tables-5.2A & B.

The mean price relative as on the date 30 days before announcement [t-30] is 103.20 whereas the mean price relative a year after announcement [t+365] is 121.57 meaning a 17.80 per cent increase. Also notable is that the coefficient of variation increased by around 2.82 times from a mere 0.17 at t-30 to 0.48 at t+365. Since the 'F' ratio [5.187] is significant the null hypothesis is not acceptable. It implies that the price relatives at different time points are significantly different from each other and do not share common characteristics. Also, they are not from the same population. This would suggest that bonus issues have influenced share prices, bonus being a common variable for all the observations in our sample.

Table - 5.2A

Descriptive Statistics of Price Relatives

Observation	Mean	St.Dev	Co-efficient of variation
t-30	103.20	17.24	0.17
t-15	104.85	18.87	0.18
t	110.48	20.50	0.19
t+15	109.77	24.59	0.22
t+30	110.29	27.94	0.28
t+90	110.72	32.26	0.29
t+180	121.71	45.56	0.37
t+270	123.50	53.35	0.43
t+365	121.57	58.47	0.48

Table - 5.2B

One Way Analysis of Variance of Price Relatives

Source	Sum of Squares	D.F.	Mean Square	'F' Ratio
Between	54592.654	8	6824.082	5.187
Within	1420800.315	1080	1315.556	
Total	1475392.969	1088	Critical Value = 2.51*	

* Critical value at $\alpha = 0.01$

Therefore, it is now necessary to further investigate into the nature and extent of differences among the observations to highlight the bonus implications for the market. For this purpose, we have analysed the price relatives 1. over the entire period of time and also for all the sub-periods [Time-wise analysis]; 2. for different bonus sizes [size-wise analysis]; and 3. extent of dividend change associated with the bonus issue [dividend change-wise analysis].

Table-5.3 presents time-wise analysis of average price relatives. It may be observed that the first sub-period belongs to the pre-revised bonus guidelines period, and second sub-period belongs to post-revised guidelines period with normal market conditions. The third sub-period belongs to the post-revised period with a capital market boom in the early part of sub-period. It is interesting to note that the overall average price relatives shift to a higher plane on announcement date and also on 180 days after the announcement date. The average price relative as on the announcement date for all the years stood at 110.48 whereas it was 104.85, 15 days before. In other words, the average price relative shows a 5.37 per cent [(110.48 - 104.85)/104.85] increase on announcement date over the price relative 15 days before. Similarly a 9.93 per cent increase is seen in the price relative at t+180 compared to the one at t+90. This step up in the overall market price relative may well be explained by the fact that the market immediately reacted to announcement. Before announcement date rumours might be afloat and

Table-5.3

Average Price Relatives - A Sub-Period Analysis

Period	No. of Cases	Observations as on Date								
		t-30	t-15	t	t+15	t+30	t+90	t+180	t+270	t+365
1979-80	10	103.27	104.72	108.96	109.93	109.19	108.10	106.73	104.56	101.16
σ		4.56	10.08	10.07	11.99	13.33	13.45	24.22	34.83	43.25
1981-84	40	97.17	98.70	103.12	105.52	104.58	106.48	113.17	121.60	117.66
σ		19.38	19.16	22.50	29.11	31.46	37.55	43.15	50.07	53.40
1985-88	71	106.59	108.33	114.84	112.14	113.67	113.48	128.62	127.24	126.64
σ		16.28	18.95	19.37	23.02	27.09	30.92	48.20	57.08	62.75
1979-88	121	103.20	104.85	110.48	109.77	110.29	110.72	121.50	123.50	121.57
		17.24	18.87	20.50	24.58	27.94	32.26	45.56	53.35	58.47

expectations getting built up, but the uncertainty regarding the timing and ratio of possible bonus will immediately keep the market participants in a low profile. It may be because of that the average price relative before announcement date was very marginally higher than the base date [t+90]. On announcement date bonus is no more a rumour but a fact and in the light of this, market participants start reassessing the value of the scrip. The consequence of such a reassessment will be an upward shift in the price relative on the announcement date which may be expected to remain stable until the price correction follows [which in our case happens after the time point t+90]. The next shift on t+180 may be attributable to the fact that majority of the scripts have been quoted ex-bonus and have been converted into cum-bonus prices on the basis of bonus ratio. This by implication means that the prices have not undergone full correction to the extent of bonus ratio. Once again, the price relatives 180 days after and other subsequent points of time exhibit a sort of stability. While these shifts are obvious in the second [1981-84] and third [1985-88] sub-periods, the case of the first sub-period (1979-80) is different. Initially there was an improvement in the price relative on announcement date but later got diluted close to the level of base date price relative especially 180 days after the announcement and other subsequent time points. In between the announcement date and t+90, the price relatives for this sub-period do not exhibit any extreme fluctuations. It was 108.96 on announcement date which marginally rose to 109.93 at t+15 and then, started climbing down. In the next two stages of observations [t+30 and t+90] the fall is marginal but after that it slides down to 106.73 at t+180. In spite of the bonus correction taking place in the prices at this point of time for most of the scrips, the price relative has come down for this sub-period. The apparent reason seems to be that managements did not announce their post-bonus dividend intentions. The revised guidelines insisted on a relatively certain and stable pay out behaviour on the part of corporate sector. Even though the second sub-period [1981-84] followed the overall pattern in shifts in the price relatives, it manifested a unique trend in the sense that the pre-announcement price relatives even dropped below those of the base date. A possible reason for such a trend appears to be a very cautious reaction of the market toward rumours about bonus during this period. It may be reminded that this period assumes special significance in two ways: 1. the period is like a gestation period for the market to comprehend and assimilate the implications of fresh and frequently revised guidelines which were more specific and stringent in nature; and 2. the capital market in India witnessed a depressed activity during this period. The overall price relative a year after the announcement date gained 10 points over that of announcement date and 18 points over the price relative at t-30. It is thus obvious that bonus rumours have a negligible effect on share prices, bonus announcement a marginal effect and a substantial portion of the increase in the market value of shares in the hands of an investor has come primarily from the post-bonus correction effect.

It has been an empirical conclusion both by Barker [6] and Gupta [7] that the news of bonus causes erratic fluctuations in share prices around the announcement date. We also observed that there are shifts in the price relatives at two stages, i.e., 1. on announcement and 2. after bonus correction. If the price relatives before announcement, between announcement and correction and after correction came from the same population we can conclude that there are no such wide fluctuations within the observations. It may also be observed that if the prices witness wide fluctuations the price relatives originate from a different population. We performed the ANOVA test to verify this inference by grouping t-30 and t-15 as pre-announcement observation, t, t+15, t+30 and t+90 as post-announcement but pre-correction observations; and t+180, t+270, and t+365 as post-correction observations. The results are presented in Table-5.4. It can be seen from the table that the 'F' Ratio for the post-announcement pre-correction group is significant. Hence, one cannot reject the alternate hypothesis that these samples came from different populations since their means are not equal. This implies that the price fluctuations are widely dispersed and quite possibly the result of bonus announcement and widely prevalent speculative tendencies on the part of market participants.

Table-5.4

ANOVA Result of the Grouped Observations

Source	Sum of Squares	D.F.	Mean Square	'F' Ratio	Critical Value*
A: Pre Announcement Group [t-30 & t-15]:					
Between	164.283	1	164.283	1.99	6366
Within	78406.848	240	326.695		
B: Post Announcement but Pre-Correction Group [t, t+15, t+30, and t+90]:					
Between	58.717	3	19.572	36.35	26.1
Within	341503.308	480	711.465		
C: Post-Correction Group [t+180, t+270 and t+365]:					
Between	281.985	2	140.992	19.719	99.50
Within	1000890.159	360	2780.250		

* at $\alpha = 0.01$

Table-5.5 contains information with regard to average price relatives according to five bonus size groups. The observations have been compiled as on nine time points. It can be seen from the table that a lower bonus ratio does not create very favourable market effects. For example, the bonus size class of less than or equal to 25 per cent is acually accompanied by a lower price relative after ex-date. Also, it is accompanied by a larger negative dividend advantage in percentage terms [8]. If this situation has an analogy it lies in the stock dividends of US pattern where bonus shares in this size will not lead to a full correction in the share price, so that the market value in the hands of investor would remain almost unchanged [9].

The Indian capital market scenario appears to have a stronger response to the cash component of dividends than to the bonus component. In fact, bonus issues upto 25 per cent have been found to be effecting market values even adversely. It is remarkable that the shifts observed in time series analysis are replicated in the size-wise analysis also excepting again the first group, viz., bonus size less than or equal to 25 per cent.

It is noticeable that the mean price relative of bonus size class 25%<BP<40% witnessed a very high increase after one year. For example, from a low of 104.54 at t-30 the average price relative has leaped to 140.68 at t+365. The same trend is visible in the bonus size class of 40%<BP<60%. It may be recalled that a predominant number of these bonus issues were followed by a significant increment in the dividend quantum.[10] These observations lead us to analyse the trends in price relative from the point of the associated dividend changes. These findings underline the significance of analysing trends in price relatives and the associated dividend changes. The next section contains this analysis.

Table-5.5

Average Price Relatives - A Bonus-Size-Wise-Analysis

Bonus Size [%]	No. of Cases	Observations as on Date								
		t-30	t-15	t	t+15	t+30	t+90	t+180	t+270	t+365
BP<25	13	105.04	104.19	108.14	103.82	107.09	107.73	104.18	95.86	93.33
σ		12.15	15.81	14.10	20.95	20.33	31.22	27.71	34.64	35.67
25<BP<40	22	104.54	107.44	113.86	112.15	110.76	17.75	128.70	140.08	140.68
σ		10.45	15.09	20.69	25.95	27.87	34.23	40.14	66.89	72.86
40<BP<60	24	101.88	103.27	109.69	107.79	108.99	108.85	121.02	120.23	132.44
σ		24.90	22.48	25.27	29.90	35.58	38.79	59.29	55.05	80.38
60<BP<80	22	102.81	106.00	107.79	109.15	107.54	103.94	119.52	127.55	114.73
σ		13.50	20.44	18.60	20.00	22.10	23.99	33.93	39.49	38.05
BP>80	40	102.87	103.96	111.35	111.93	113.37	112.67	125.17	123.11	117.47
σ		18.53	19.15	20.62	24.44	28.77	31.79	49.45	54.09	45.74
All	121	103.20	104.85	110.48	109.77	110.29	110.72	121.71	123.50	121.57
σ		17.24	18.87	20.50	24.59	27.94	32.26	45.46	53.35	58.47

A point to be noted is that in calculating the price relatives we could not exclude the dividend effect on prices. Obviously. the observed changes in the price relatives at different points of observations cannot completely be associated to the bonus issue alone. Therefore, it is necessary to analyse the average price relatives for different ranges of changes in post-bonus dividend quantum. Table-5.6 presents this information. Average price relatives and their standard deviations at different time points for six categories of dividend quantum changes have been shown in Table-5.6. It is clear from the data that the general pattern of price changes was in broad agreement with the pattern of dividend changes. There were three bonus issues whose post-bonus dividend quantum is less than the pre-bonus dividend quantum. For this group the average price relative after one year from announcement date plunged to a low of 73.84 from 100.68 at t-30. Same is the case for a dividend change of 0-10 per cent range. The market appears to be almost indifferent for a dividend change range of 10-20 per cent. For a dividend growth rate group of 10-20 per cent the price relative 30 days before was 99.80 and a year after it was 100.08. This for all practical purposes is no growth at all. Another interesting point to be noted is that the percentage increment in price relative a year after the bonus announcement is always less than the percentage increment in the dividend quantum. It suggests that dividend increase greatly exceeded the price gain in all the categories. Thus it can be concluded that the market is not really assigning any special significance to bonus issue *'per se'* in the valuation process but to the expected attendant changes in the more fundamental variables like dividends. This conclusion can further be explained through rank correlation.

Table - 5.6

Post-Bonus Dividend Change - Average Price Relatives

Dividend	No. of	Observations as on Date								
Quantum	Cases	t-30	t-15	t	t+15	t+30	t+90	t+180	t+270	t+365
<0	3	100.68	100.79	99.79	99.18	98.38	103.36	88.37	79.97	73.84
σ		3.30	2.69	2.62	2.84	3.91	23.37	1.95	5.96	3.81
0-10	4	89.97	88.01	96.33	90.06	89.94	80.50	91.59	66.12	73.64
σ		27.19	27.85	30.99	38.51	40.21	33.39	67.25	28.67	26.26
10-20	27	99.80	98.51	103.28	101.62	102.68	103.23	103.93	106.08	100.08
σ		16.23	16.65	21.33	24.63	29.84	35.64	38.46	35.76	39.80
20-30	22	103.70	106.18	109.45	102.23	102.30	105.06	115.26	123.90	122.58
σ		13.72	15.24	17.42	23.68	26.43	27.69	36.02	59.45	54.10
30-50	52	104.77	108.06	114.09	116.57	116.88	116.40	135.69	132.37	136.23
σ		19.38	21.35	20.96	24.18	27.58	33.74	51.21	49.84	67.75
>50	13	107.80	109.05	119.59	120.79	122.28	124.13	130.55	150.95	131.60
σ		13.00	12.89	14.78	12.27	15.76	16.21	26.61	73.24	50.36

In Table-5.7 we present the rank correlation matrix for price relatives. The correlation coefficients clearly show a declining trend as we move farther from the base set. This will happen when we move down vertically and move left-wards horizontally on the matrix. The rank correlation between the observations 30 days before announcement and a year after is just 0.26764; and between the announcement day observations and a year there after the rank correlation is 0.61338. A point that emerges from the rank correlation matrix is that two immediate sets have a high coefficient of correlation but as the time span for observations increases it gradually declines.

V. Regression Result

Table-5.8 portrays the results of the regressions performed with and without the bonus as an independent variable in our log-linear model. The bonus has been included as a dummy variable in the sets of observations at different points of time. Different values for the dummy variable have been worked by pooling each time period with the base date [t-90]. It is clear from the table that the 'F' Ratio has consistently been higher than the critical value and is highly significant. Also, the values of R^2 (adjusted) have been consistently high. These results affirm the explanatory power of the model. It is, however, to be noted that inclusion of bonus as an independent variable in the model, marginally reduced the explanatory power of the regression in the first two sets of pooled observations. The R^2 (Adjusted) in the first set of pooled observations [t-90+t-30] is .67548 when bonus is included as a variable and is less than that when it is not included [.6763]. Similarly it got reduced to 0.6778 from 0.6781 with the second set of pooled observations [t-90+t-15]. From announcement date onwards bonus as an independent variable improved the performance of the model as is evident from the fact that R^2 (Adjusted) of inclusive regression is more than the exclusive regression.

Table-5.7

Rank Correlation Matrix for Price Relatives

	t-30	t-15	t	t+15	t+30	t+90	t+180	t+270
t-30	1.00000							
t-15	.82669	1.00000						
t	.68779	.77734	1.00000					
t+15	.50031	.58697	.76563	1.00000				
t+30	.49742	.56879	.74005	.95097	1.00000			
t+90	.40152	.43121	.61338	.76696	.82704	1.0000		
t+180	.38988	.38479	.54312	.61007	.64623	.71761	1.00000	
t+270	.32737	.33801	.48326	.53661	.56396	.62158	.83561	1.00000
t+365	.29764	.33720	.45262	.49917	.51227	.59769	.78873	.87168

Critical value (1-Tail, .05) = + Or - .15031

Critical Value (2-tall, .05) = +/- .17853 N = 121

In Table-5.9 we present the coefficients, Standard error and T. ratios of the independent variables in the bonus inclusive pooled regression. All variables except 'β_6' are significant at α=0.05. Even the bonus variable turns significant after t+90 at α=0.01. It will be seen from the various beta values in table-5.9 that 'β' for dividend variable emerges as a very important determinant of the share values at all the nine points of time. The high values of 'T Ratios' confirm this belief. The variable next in importance is growth with relatively similar values for 'T Ratios'. Risk as a determinant of share prices again emerges as a powerful and significant variable and inversely affects the market value of shares. The negative sign is expected and the value of T.Ratios though not very high indicate the coefficient to be significant.

Table-5.8

Overall Significance of Regression

t-90 pooled with	β_0	R^2 (Adjusted)	Stand. error	'F' ratio
t-30	.3560	.6755	.2800	84.61
*	.3613	.6763	.27960	101.70
t-15	.3732	.6778	.2783	85.51
*	.3793	.6781	.2782	102.54
t	.3746	.6875	.2714	89.37
*	.3846	.6855	.2723	106.07
t+15	.4118	.6627	.2826	79.91
*	.4190	.6613	.2832	95.11
t+30	.4132	.6603	.2838	79.08
*	.4183	.6589	.2844	94.13
t+90	.3783	.6650	.2818	80.75
*	.3777	.6630	.2827	95.83
t+180	.3327	.6767	.2789	85.06
*	.3093	.6676	.2828	97.80
t+270	.3565	.6664	.2861	81.23
*	.3091	.6550	.2910	92.50
t+365	.3584	.6767	.2838	85.09
*	.2864	.6656	.2886	96.93

* **Regression result when bonus is not included as an independent variable.**

F = 2.80 [D.F=6,236 & α=0.01]

*F =320 [D.F-5, 236 & α=0.01]

Our main concern is to examine the positioning and role of bonus variable as a determinant of share prices in this multi regression analysis. The results contained in Table-5.9 clearly point out that the value of bonus coefficients is both low and insignificant [α=0.01] upto the time point t+90. The coefficient turns significant at t+180 and remains so at increasing level upto t+365. It may be mentioned that since most of the shares were quoted ex-bonus at t+180 we adjusted to cum-bonus prices with a view to maintaining the consistency in price data for nine time points. It must further be observed that since the diluted prices have not undergone the full bonus correction the shareholders might have gained in terms of higher share prices. This phenomenon is in full conformity with the conclusions of Woolridge, J.R.,[11] who

Table-5.9

Regression Result of the Independent Variables

Sets		Dividend	Growth	Risk	Size	Market	Bonus
t-30	Co-Effi	0.75830	0.60876	-0.76178	0.10230	0.33993	0.02323
	St.Error	0.04481	0.31165	0.18609	0.03824	0.08226	0.03605
	T Ratio	16.92200	1.95300	-4.09400	2.67500	4.13200	0.64400
t-15	Co-Effi	0.75910	0.65400	-0.75760	0.09950	0.33540	0.03180
	St.Error	0.04460	0.30990	0.18500	0.03810	0.08190	0.03590
	T Ratio	17.02300	2.11000	-4.09500	2.61000	4.09800	0.88700
t	Co-Effi	0.75370	0.60060	-0.76120	0.10160	0.33490	0.05530
	St. Error	0.04350	0.30210	0.18040	0.03720	0.08000	0.03500
	T Ratio	17.33200	1.98900	-4.22000	2.73000	4.18500	1.58100
t+15	Co-Effi	0.74050	0.74930	-0.72310	0.11310	0.30270	0.05090
	St.Error	0.04530	0.31440	0.18760	0.03860	0.08340	0.03640
	T Ratio	16.36100	2.38300	-3.85400	2.92600	3.62900	1.39600
t+30	Co-Effi	0.74710	0.69370	-0.70640	0.10140	0.31900	0.05130
	St.Error	0.04550	0.32600	0.18820	0.03880	0.08410	0.03660
	T Ratio	16.42800	2.19500	-3.75400	2.61200	3.79300	1.40100
t+90	Co-Effi	0.74970	0.74470	-0.68390	0.10190	0.33050	0.05690
	St.Error	0.04510	0.31440	0.18660	0.03850	0.08260	0.03650
	T Ratio	16.60800	2.36900	-3.66400	2.64400	4.00000	1.56000
t+180	Co-Effi	0.75610	0.82860	-0.64930	0.09960	0.34840	0.10030
	St.Error	0.04440	0.31150	0.18470	0.03800	0.08640	0.03630
	T Ratio	17.01500	2.66000	-3.51400	2.61700	4.17600	2.76200
t+270	Co-Effi	0.76010	0.78720	-0.60320	0.10580	0.33110	0.11300
	St.Error	0.04560	0.31970	0.19040	0.03890	0.08570	0.03750
	T Ratio	16.65500	2.46200	-3.16700	2.71800	3.86400	3.01200
t+365	Co-Effi	0.78380	0.83380	-0.53900	0.09910	0.33330	0.11360
	St.Error	0.04530	0.31690	0.18880	0.03860	0.08550	0.03760
	T Ratio	17.29100	2.63100	-2.85500	2.56800	3.89600	3.02500

associates this inability of the market to fully adjust the price on ex-date to the presence of imperfections, inefficiencies or both. In fact all the three reasons i.e., indivisibility, taxes and transactions costs, that were identified by him as indicators of imperfections are very much present in the Indian Capital market and one might see them impinging too hard on the correction process. Till the ex-date [t+180] the market has not considered bonus issue [rumour or announcement] as an active independent variable in the process of price determination. It must be stated that the coefficient values for the bonus variable within the time range t to t+90 are significant only at $\alpha=0.20$. This implies that the market has ignored bonus as an active variable influencing prices. It is only at t+180 and thereafter that the bonus coefficient turns significant at $\alpha=0.01$. This being the ex-date the fact of bonus as an established element in the information rapporteur of the market is immediately absorbed in the market valuation process. This finding derives strength from Jandhyala's result of an empirical study which found Indian capital market to be informationally efficient.[12]

Table-5.10

Residuals and 'F' Ratios for the Test of Coincidence

Observations	Σe^2_p	Σe^2_o	'F' Ratio
	[D.F. =230,6]		
t-30	18.45	9.26	5.32
t-15	18.27	9.09	5.93
t	17.50	8.21	2.38
t+15	18.93	9.64	2.57
t+30	19.08	9.81	2.74
t+90	18.86	9.52	2.02
	[D.F. = 6,230]		
t+180	18.87	9.09	1.43
t+270	19.98	10.05	1.66
t+365	19.66	9.65	1.85

$\Sigma e^2_b=9.10$ Critical value at $\alpha=0.01$

'F' Ratio [D.F. 230,6] = 6.88

'F' Ratio [D.F. 6,230] = 2.80

The regression result based on the bonus inclusive pooled observations, thus, indicate that bonus is not considered as a significant independent variable in the valuation equation but for the presence of inefficiencies, imperfections or both in the Indian Capital Market. The holding value of the shares has increased due to partial correction for bonus as the transaction costs, taxes and indivisibility of shares exist in the market. In over all terms rumours or announcement of bonus decision seems to have no sustained and significant effect on the share prices.

The observation made regarding the bonus assuming significance as an independent variable due to the presence of inefficiency and imperfections in the capital market and not bonus *'per se'* can further be explained through a test of coincidence. In Table-5.10 we present the residuals of pooled and individual samples along with the 'F' Ratios. These are the residuals of regressions run with 5 independent variables, viz., dividend, growth, risk, size, and market. As is apparent from the table 'F' Ratio is significant for none of the sets. This implies that there is no change in the valuation process either before or after bonus announcement. The result of the test of coincidence. thus, states that issue of bonus shares *'per se'* is not considered of any consequence for the share price.

Our hypothesis that unless bonus shares are followed by an increase in the cash quantum of dividend will not generally increase the value of shares in the market is acceptable since the result of price relative analysis, regression analysis and coincidence test support our hypothesis. Generally speaking, little evidence is found that will support the belief that bonus pays off with higher prices. This, however, cannot be considered as stating that market price will not increase. The result simply shows that, in general, share prices after bonus issue are not significantly higher than it would have been if it is not done. However, this does not rule out the possibility of bonus issue being associated with some beneficial effects on shares of some specific companies. Also there could be a possibility of share prices recording losses possibly because there has been a net reduction in the dividend quantum after bonus or because of some other fundamental factors turning against the company.

VI. Summary and Findings

The purpose of this chapter is to assess if bonus shares have any beneficial or detrimental effect on share prices. For this purpose we analysed the price trends of 121 bonus issues of 79 companies. This was done by examining the price trends broadly in two ways: 1. analysis of price relatives and 2. statistical significance of bonus as an independent variable in a multi variate regression model of equity share valuation. The major findings of this analysis may be outlined as under:

1. Share prices underwent significant changes after the issue of bonus shares. The average price relative 30 days before announcement was just 103.20 whereas 365 days after announcement it was 121.57.

2. The bonus issues that are made after the revision of guidelines appear to have had a beneficial impact on share prices rather than those related to before that period.

3. The prices in between the announcement date and 90 days there after seem to have witnessed wide fluctuations. The mean price relatives at different time points between these dates do not have

identical means and the null hypothesis that they came from the same population is rejected.

4. The average price relatives of various bonus size classes have shown an increasing trend for the bonus size class of 25 per cent and above.

5. The aggregate average price relatives have shown an upward swing on announcement date and also on and after 180 days. [the day on which large number of sample shares are quoted ex-bonus]. Between these shifts the price relatives manifested a near stability.

6. It has been observed that the increase in the average price relatives after the announcement and a year there after is always less than that in the dividend quantum. This may be interpreted to mean that the sustenance of growth in price is due to the increase in dividend quantum. This is apparent if one observes the price trend of those issues that have followed with a dividend quantum increase of less than 10 per cent. In such of the cases where the dividend quantum growth is less than 10 per cent the price relatives have tumbled down to an average of 73 per cent. This only means that bonus *'per se'* is seen as of no vlaue.

7. The above conclusion that price rise is not due to bonus issue is further explained by rank correlation of price relatives. The rank correlation, though all through positive, has weakened as the time span between observations increased. It suggests that price relatives do not have a sustained position.

8. Bonus as an independent variable became significant only for those observations related to the period when price dilution took place. The shareholder seems to have gained due to partial correction for bonus in prices.

9. Our test of coincidence does not reveal any change in the manner of equity valuation after bonus issue from that of the pre-bonus period.

It can, thus, be concluded that the increase in the share price, though apparently associated with the bonus issue, cannot possibly be attributed to it. Share price increase in most of the situations is a consequence of the post-bonus changes in other variables particularly the dividend quantum.

References

1. David Durand, Modiglioni & Miller, Gordon, Henishay, Fisher, Weston, Barges, Friend & Puckett, Raj Ojha, Prasanna Chandra.

2. M.M., assert that in a perfect market setting leverage has no effect on the value of the firm. It is considered as a 'superfluous' variable in the Indian context by Prasanna Chandra.

3a. Markowitz, H.M., Portfolio Selection-Efficient Diversification of Investments, New York, John Weiley & Sons inc., 1959;

3b. Markowitz, H.M., Portfolio Selection, The Journal of Finance, Vol. 12 (March, 52) pp. 77-91;

3c. Sharpe, W.F., A Simplified Model for Portfolio Analysis, The Management Science, Vol. 9, No. 3 (Jan 63), pp. 277-293.

4. Walter, Gorden and other

5. Chow, G.C., Test of Equality Between Sets of Co- efficients in Two Linear Regressions, Econometrica, Vol.28, 1960, pp. 591-605.

6. .... there is a strong but short lived price run up during the first few days after news of stock dividend reaches the public, particularly when the dividend is special, non periodic and unexpected by the investor

7. Bonus issue decisions almost invariably result in an immediate price rise of a fairly significant order...

8. See Table-4.8 in Chapter-IV.

9. Para 5.4 in Chapter-II.

10. See para 4.4 in chapter-IV.

11. para 4.16 in chapter-I

12. Jandhyala L. Sharma, Efficient Capital Markets and Random Character of Stock Price Behaviour in a Developing Economy, Indian Journal of Economics, Vol. LXIII, (April, 1983), Issue No. 251, pp. 365-419.

VI

Summary and Findings

The Hypothesis

There is consensus on the equity share price valuation process being influenced considerably by the future expected net cash flows. In fact, the fundamentalists assert that the market price of equity shares will at any point of time be the discounted value of the future expected net cash flows from resources invested in equity shares. The discount rate is often the rate of return required by the investors. An assumption which goes behind such a view is that the markets are competitive and both volume of trading and the number of participants are adequate to keep the market alive. Nevertheless, operators in the market have been reported to be enlarging their gains by capitalising on cosmetic events like issue of bonus shares, associated rumours and other such non-fundamental factors. It may be added that a bonus share does not alter the net-worth position of the company so that its intrinsic value does not also change. However, a bonus share becomes of considerable value if it provides enlarged future net cash flows in the form of increased dividend quantum on a larger number of shares which an investor is allotted in the event of a bonus decision by a company. It is, therefore, not very surprising that the bulk of the studies centered on the theme of exploring a relationship between the bonus shares and the value of the equity have concluded that bonus *'per se'* is of no consequence to the investor. The moment a bonus is announced the market begins to pulsate in its speculations about the future course of events. Immediate psychological effect is that a company issuing bonus shares will do so only when it can at least maintain the dividend quantum and there is no possibility of the total future expected dividend shrinking. This kind of market sentiment has the immediate effect of pushing up share prices when the bonus event takes place. The duration of such increase may range from excessively short to the date of formal announcement of official sanction reaching the market. Operators who capitalise on such a cosmetic event are able to book profits in the short run. It must also be added that the rise in the price in the wake of 'bonus rumours' is seldom in the proportion of a bonus ratio and this will be true even when the market is just guessing about the bonus issue. At the same time this is also true when the correction process starts after the bonus scrips are issued or in some cases even before that. It must be noted that from day one to day 'n' the fundamental factors continue to operate. The way they get mixed up with the cosmetic events it is difficult to delineate. Hence, a very absolute and clear conclusion does not often emerge.

This study is aimed at underlining if bonus shares issued by the Indian private corporate sector during the period 1977-88 have given raise to a real gain to the investors. In this pursuit we also investigated into the general characteristic features of bonus issues made during the study period. We have also analysed the post-bonus dividends since it is considered to be the most powerful determinant of the value in the Indian context. As a prelude to this analysis we described the theoretical and legal underpinnings which provided a basis for our subsequent analysis. Thus, the whole debate of this study centered around the broad theme whether bonus shares were of any investment value to the shareholders. After a detailed review of the existing empirical studies in this area we formulated the following hypothesis:

> *"Bonus shares will not generally increase the value of shares in the market unless followed by an increase in the cash quantum of dividend. The usual phenomenon of market price-run up in anticipation of or in the wake of rumours about bonus issues is primarily caused by a higher dividend pay out [not necessarily ratio] expectations of the market."*

The Data and Method of Analysis

We have included 435 bonus issues made by 259 companies during the period 1977-88. The companies covered have their registered offices in India and are listed on Bombay Stock Exchange. To analyse the exclusive price consequences of bonus issues we included only such bonus issues that are not associated with any concurrent or simultaneous dividend announcement. The choice of the period 1977-88 is primarily influenced by the corporate investment behaviour acquiring a new surge after a series of set backs since the commencement of Fourth Five year plan and during the plan holiday period. The bonus issues made after 1976 have been included with a view to avoiding a possible spill-over effect of the Dividend Restriction Ordinance, 1974 which was repealed during 1975.

For delineating the characteristic features of bonus issues by the Indian private corporate sector during 1977-88 we have used all the 435 bonus issues by 259 companies. To analyse the post-bonus dividend tracks, the information constraint regarding the dividend details restricted our sample to 415 issues made by 249 companies. To investigate into the valuation effects of bonus issues we used 121 bonus issues of 79 companies. Non-availability of announcement dates, non-existence of Bombay Stock Exchange sensitive Index, non-frequent trading of the scrip or non-listing of the scrip on Bombay Stock Exchange have limited our sample to 121 for this purpose.

The major sources of information have been the Bombay Stock Exchange Directory and Bombay Stock Exchange Official Price Quotations. The details regarding the announcement dates of some bonus issues have been gathered from the companies through administering the 'INFORMATION SCHEDULE' and for others we have drawn the information from the Bombay Stock Exchange files. Where ever the financial year differed from 12 month period the data relating to that year has been annualised so as to bring in comparability in the data. The closing price is used to analyse the bonus effects on price. When the price on any required date is not available due to that date being a non-trading day or the scrip not being traded on that date, the price data available immediately preceding that date has been used.

The structure and design of the study may now be briefly outlined. The first chapter [INTRODUCTION] discusses the problem into which investigation has been attempted in this study, lays down the objectives of the study and also specifies its scope. In addition, it also contains a review of existing empirical studies in the area of bonus shares in India and its equivalent in the US and highlights the specific issues addressed by such studies. The hypothesis to be tested has also been specified in this chapter. A brief outline of the methodology followed in the study has also been attempted. The chapter concludes with a description of the plan of this study.

Chapter-II [BONUS SHARES - THEORETICAL AND LEGAL UNDERPINNINGS] attempts to delineate the conceptual and legal aspects related to bonus shares. An extensive discussion on the nature of bonus shares is followed by a comparison of bonus shares with sub-divided shares, stock dividends, stock splits and rights shares. It also covers the procedures involved in the issue of bonus shares and highlights, *inter alia*, the critical legal issues related to them. This chapter concludes with a brief discussion on the tax implications of bonus shares.

A description of the characteristic features of bonus shares issued by the Indian private corporate sector is discussed in Chapter-III [BONUS SHARES - AN EMPIRICAL RETROSPECT]. It covers the number, frequency, time interval between bonus issues, ratios and amount of bonus issues, the size of the companies making bonus issues and the extent of capitalisation of reserves by them. The analysis includes time-wise and industry-wise analysis.

The summary of the findings of this analysis is given toward the end of this chapter.

What happened to the post-bonus dividend pay-out is the focal point for analysis in Chapter-IV [BONUS SHARES - DIVIDEND CHANGES]. We have used two parameters to analyse the extent of post-bonus dividend changes: viz., the magnitude of dividend change and the dividend advantage. The magnitude of dividend change is the change in the post-bonus dividend quantum relative to the pre-bonus dividend quantum. The dividend advantage is the percentage of pre-bonus dividend quantum given to the shareholders after the issue of bonus shares on the capitalised amount. In this chapter an analysis of direction of changes in dividend rates and quantum have been undertaken. In addition, an attempt to examine the pre and post-bonus tracks of dividend quantum changes to highlight the association of such changes in bonus year to bonus issues is also made. This chapter ends with a brief summary of findings of our analysis.

Having discussed the theoretical and legal underpinnings related to the issue of bonus shares in India, and having observed the characteristics features of bonus issues made by the Indian private corporate sector and the dividend changes that follow, the stage was set to examine the valuation effects of bonus issues. The analysis of such effects is covered in Chapter-V [VALUATION EFFECTS OF BONUS SHARES]. We considered the prices at ten different time points, i.e., 90 days, 30 days, 15 days before announcement date, announcement date, 15 days, 30 days, 90 days, 180 days, 270 days and 365 days after announcement date. We followed two approaches to analyse the bonus implications on the price, viz., 1. price relative analysis and 2. statistical significance of bonus issue as an independent variable determining the price. We attempted to observe the effects of bonus issues on the basis of price relatives which have been calculated using the price and Bombay Stock Exchange Sensitive Index as on 90 days before announcement date as base. This has been done with an assumption that the market is affected not even by the rumours about the forth-coming bonus issue. The price relative analysis has been done according to the period, bonus size and the post-bonus dividend changes. Using dividend, growth rate, risk, size and market index as independent variables in a log-linear regression share valuation model we tested the statistical significance of bonus issue as an independent variable in two ways, i.e., 1. bonus represented by a, zero-one dummy variable in the valuation model and 2. test of coincidence. The last section of the chapter is a summary of findings based on the analysis conducted in this part of the study.

The last chapter [SUMMARY AND CONCLUSIONS] contains a summary of the entire study.

Empirical Findings

The Indian corporate sector continued to favour capitalisation of reserves in certain high ratios like 1:1, 3:5, 1:2, and 2:5. Majority of the bonus issues have been made immediately after the expiry of minimum time gap between two bonus issues specified by the guidelines. Liberalisation measures initiated after 1985 along with the boom in the capital market appear to have encouraged the corporate sector to capitalise the reserves as a consequence of which there was a spurt in the bonus issues both in number and amount after 1985. It is also found that the small and medium companies accounted for a major chunk of capitalisation of reserves during the same period. The corporate sector manifested in aggregate a measured inaggressiveness in capitalisation of its reserves and the guideline relating to the residual reserves made redundant. The firms in the industry groups classified 'public utility' and/or 'under-price-controls' show a tendency of non-frequent and conservative approach to capitalisation of reserves.

An overwhelming majority of bonus issues followed an increased dividend quantum in the bonus year. The range of increase in the dividend quantum was almost equivalent to the bonus ratio in all such cases.

The results of price relative analysis, regression analysis and coincidence test show that bonus *'per se'* has no effect on the value of the firm. This conclusion is arrived because of two reasons: 1. the increase in the price relative is almost always less than the increase in the dividend quantum and 2. it is because of the partial correction in the share price that bonus as an independent variable in the log-linear multiple regression model became significant at a time point 180 days from the announcement date and there after also. This partial correction is primarily attributable to the presence of imperfections, inefficience or both in the Indian capital market. *Thus, the results of our empirical analysis do not refute our hypothesis and provide positive evidence to state that the issue of bonus shares does not act as a variable having a positive influence on the value of the firm but for the ex-post changes in the 'other' and 'more fundamental' variables especially in the subsequent dividend quantum.*

This, however, cannot be considered as stating that market price will not increase. The result simply shows that, in general, share prices after bonus issue are not significantly higher than it would have been if there had been no bonus.

Further Research

There is a need and scope for further research in this area so that the true role of bonus variable can be further focused in the overall equity share valuation context. This will help comprehending the underpinnings of actual market operations as well. The questions in particular to be posed for further research on the subject may be formulated as below:

1. Why companies continue to issue bonus shares despite the negative conclusions of so many empirical studies here and abroad, is a common question asked by any practitioner. To answer this usual query one need to probe into the motivations and expectations of managements in issuing the bonus shares. It is equally important to analyse the extent to which these expectations have been realised through bonus issues by those companies.

2. Why are the investors crazy about bonus shares and what really affects them to manifest such a behaviour when bonus is on anvil. For this one need to classify the investors into some common groups depending on their investment objectives and delineate the extent to which issue of bonus shares contributes to their objective.

3. Examining the extent of 'excess returns' with reference to different time-points to identify the possibility of booking profits due to announcement of bonus shares is another aspect requiring further research.

4. A model incorporating the residual reserves, volume of trading, post-bonus paid up equity capital, post-bonus growth in expected earnings, and post-bonus pay-out behaviour of the companies may be attempted to better explain the price behaviour around and after announcement and ex-date. This will be of great help in underlining the set of conditions under which bonus be of value.

5. Finally, a methodological suggestion can be offered with regard to further research in this area. A number of empirical studies have been undertaken in the USA using the 'event-time' methodology which helps in a better understanding of the speed of adjustment in share prices to the new information [be it bonus announcement or other information]. Such a methodology can be replicated using Indian capital market data also. However, the methodology requires an assessment of 'excess returns' on daily basis so that the chances of price gains because of cosmetic events are identified. It is obvious that such a study will have to be embarked upon when data on daily prices and returns is made systematically available.

Bibliography

"Agarwal, K.P.", "Equity Price Behaviour in India Since 1951-52", "Indian Journal of Economics, Vol. 46 (July 1965)", "pp. 63-92"

"Aharony, J., and Swary, I", "Quarterly Dividend and Earnings Announcements and Stockholders' Returns: An Empirical Analysis", "Journal of Finance, vol. 35 (1980)", "pp. 1-12"

"Akerlof, G.", "The Market for `lemons': Quality Uncertainty and the Market Mechanism", "Quarterly Journal of Economics, Vol 84 (1970),", "pp. 448-500"

"Arditti, Fred d.", "Risk and the Required Return on Equity", "Journal of Finance, Vol. 22 (March 1967)", "pp. 19-36"

"Asquith, P. and Mullins, D", "The Impact of Initiating Dividend Payments on shareholders' Wealth", "Journal of Business, Vol. 56 (1983)", "pp. 77-96"

"Atiase, R.", "Predisclosure, Informational Asymmetries, Firm Capitalisation, Financial Reports and Security Price Behaviour", "Unpublished Doctoral Dissertation (University of California)","

"Banz, R.W.", "The Relationship Between Return and Market Value of Common Stocks", "Journal of financial Economics, Vol.9 (1981)", "pp. 3-18"

"Bar-Yosef, S and Brown, L.", " A Re-Examination of Stock Splits Using Moving Betas", "Journal of Finance, Vol. 32 (1977)", "pp. 1069-1080"

"Barges, A.", "The Effect of Capital Structure on the Cost of Capital", "Englewood Cliffs, N.J.: Prentice Hall", "1963"

"Barker, C.A.","Evaluation of Stock Dividends", "Harvard Business Review, July-August 1958", "pp. 99-114"

"Barker, C.A.", "Price Changes of Stock Dividend at Ex-Dividend date","Journal of Finance, September 1959", "pp. 372-378"

"Barker, C.A.", "Effective Stock Splits", "Harvard Business Review, (January/Februar 1956)", "pp. 101-106"

"Beaver, W.H.", "The Information Content of Annual Earnings Announcements", "Empirical Research in Accounting: Selected Studies, 1968", "pp. 67-92"

"Bellemore, Douglas H. and Mrs. Lillian Blucher", "A Study of Stock Splits in the Post War Years", "Financial Analysts Journal, Vol. XV (Nov. 1956)", "pp. 19-26"

"Benishay, Haskell", "Variability in Earnings -Price Ratios of Corporate Equities", "American Economic Review, Vol. 51 (March 1961)", "pp. 81-94"

"Bhattacharya, S.", "Imperfect Information, Dividend Policy and `The Bird in The Hand' fallacy", "Bell Journal of Economics, Vol 12 (1979)", "pp. 259-270"

"Bombay Stock Exchange, Bombay", "Stock Exchange Official directory"

"Boness,J., Jew, Frank", "A Model of Information Diffusion, Stock Market Behaviour and Equilibrium Prices", "Journal of finance and Quantitative Analysis, vol. 5 (1970)", "pp. 274-296"

"Bothwell, J.C.", "Periodic Stock Dividends", "Harvard Business Review, January, 1950", "pp. 89-100"

"Box, G.E.P. and Pierce, A.A.", "Distribution of Residual Autocorrelations in Autoregressive Integrated Moving Average Time series Model", "Journal of American Statistical Association, Vol. 64 (1970)"

"Brickley, J.", "Shareholders Wealth, Information Signalling and the Specially Designated Dividend", "Journal of Financial Economics, vol. 12 (1983)", "pp. 187-209"

"Bringham, E. and James Pappas", "Duration of Growth, Changes in Growth Rates and Corporate Share Prices", "Financial Analysts Journal, Vol. 22 (May - June 1966)", "pp. 157-162"

"Brown, P., Kleidon, A., and Marsh, T.", "New Evidence on the Nature of Size-Related Anomalies in Stock Prices", "Journal of Financial Economics, Vol. 12 (1980)", "pp. 33-55"

"Brown, S. and Warner, J", "Measuring Security Price Performance", "Journal of Financial Economics, Vol. 8 (1980)", "pp. 205-258"

"Brown, S.J. and Warner. J.B.", "Using Daily Stock Returns: The Case of Event Studies", "Journal of Financial Economics, Vol. 14 (1985)", "pp. 13-31"

"Chandra, Prasanna", "Comparison of the Additive and Multiplicative Models of Stock Valuation", "Decision, January 1977", "pp. 45-52"

"Chandra, Prasanna", "Valuation of Equity Shares in India", "Sultan Chand and Sons", "New Delhi"

"Charest, G.", "Split Information, Stock Returns, and Market Efficiency", "Journal of Financial Economics, Vol. 6 (1978)", "pp. 265-296"

"Choi, D and Strong, R", "The Pricing of When-Issued Common Stock: A Note", "Journal of Finance, Vol. 38 (1983)", "pp. 1293-1298"

"Chottiner, Sherman and Allan Young", "A Test of the AICPA Differentiation Between Stock Dividend and Stock Splits", "Journal of Accounting Research, Vol. 9 (1971)", "pp. 367-374"

"Cohen, Jerome B. and Edward D. Zinbarg", "Investment Analysis and Portfolio Management", "Irwin", "1967"

"Committee On Accounting Procedure", "Accounting Research and Terminology Bulletins", "American Institute of Certified Public Accountants", " 1961"

"Constantinides, George M.", "Optimal Stock Trading With Porsonal Taxes", "Journal of Financial Economics, vol. 13 (1984)", "pp. 65-89"

"Cootner, P.H. (ed.)", "The Random character of Stock Prices", "(Cambridge, Mass: M.I.T. Press)", "1964"

"Copeland, T.", "Liquidity changes following stock splits", "Journal of finance, Vol. 34 (March, 1979)", "pp. 115-141"

"Copeland, thomas E. and J.F. Weston", "Financial Theory and coporate Policy, 2nd Ed.", "Addison - Wesley, Reading, MA", "1984"

"Dann, L.", "Common Stock Repurchases: An Analysis of Returns to Bondholders and Stockholders", "Journal of Financial Economics, Vol. 9 (1981)", "pp. 113-138"

"Davidson, S., Stickney, C., and Weil, R.", "Financial Accounting: An Introduction to Concepts, Methods, and Uses", "Dryden Press: Hindsdale. IL",""

"Desai, Meghnad", "Stock Prices, Earnings and Dividends in India: A Quantitative Analysis", "Indian Economic Journal, Vol. 12 (April June 1963)", "pp. 432-436"

"Dohr. J.L.", "Taxability of Stock Dividends: U.S. Supreme Court Decisions", "Journal of Accountancy, May 1943", "pp. 466-468"

"Eades, K.", "Empirical Evidence on Dividends as a Signal of Firm Value", "Journal of Financial and Quantitative Analysis, Vol 17 (1982)", "pp. 471-502"

"Eades, K., Bess, P. and Kim, H.", "On Interpreting Security Returns During the Ex-dividend Period", "Journal of Financial Economics, Vol. 13 (1984)", "pp. 3-34"

"Eisemann, P.C. and Moses, E.A.", "Stock Dividens" Managements' View", "Financial Analysts Journal, (1978)", "pp. 77-80"

"Ezekiel, Mordecai and Karl A. Fox", "Methods of Correlation and Regression Analysis,", "New York, John Wiley and Sons", "1959"

"Fama, E.F.", "Portfolio Analysis in a Stable Parentian Market", "Management Science, Vol XI (January 1965)", "pp. 404 - 419"

"Fama, E.F., Lawrence Fisher, Jensen, M.C. and Roll, R.", "The Adjustment of Stock Prices to New Information", "International Economic Review, Vol. 10, No. 1 (February, 1969)", pp. 1-21"

"Fama, E., and Macbeth, J.", "Risk Return, and Equilibrium: Empirical Tests", "Journal of Political Economy, Vol. 81 (1973)", "pp. 607-636"

"Fama, E.F.", "Risk Return and Equilibrium : Some Clarifying Comments", "Journal of Finance, Vol. 23 (March 1968)", "pp. 29-40"

"Fama, E.F.", "The Behaviour of Stock-Market Prices", "Journal of Business, Vol. 38 (January 1965)", "pp. 34-105"

"Fama, E.F.", "Efficient Capital Markets: A Review of Theory and Empirical Work", "Journal of Finance, (May 1970)", "pp. 301-417"

"Fama. E.F.", "Foundations of Finance", "Basic Books, New York", "1976"

"Fama, E.F. and Merton H.M.", "The Theory of Finance, New York", "Holt Rinehart and Winston", "1972"

"Fisher. G.", "Some Factors Influencing Share Prices", "Economic Journal, Vol. 71 (1966)", "pp. 121-141"

"Friend, Irwin J., and Marshall Puckett", "Dividends and Stock Prices", "American Economic Review, Vol. 54 (September 1964)", "pp. 656-682"

"Gordon, M.J.", "The Optimum Dividend Rate", "Management Science: Models and Techniques, London: Pergamon Press", "1960"

"Gordon, M.J.", "The Savings Investment and Valuation of a Corporation", "Review of Economics and Statistics, Vol. 44 (February 1962)", "pp. 37-51"

"Gordon, M.J.", "The Investment Financing and Valuation of Corporation", "Homewood, III.: Richard D. Irwin", "1962"

"Gordon, M.J.", "Dividends, Earnings and Stock Prices", "Review of Economic and Statistics, vol. XLI (may 1959)", "pp. 99-105"

"Grinblatt, M.S., Masulis, R.W., and Titman, S.", "The Valuation Effects of Stock Splits and Stock Dividends", "Journal of Financial Economics, Vol. 13 (1984)", "pp. 461-490"

"Gupta, U.L.", "Working of Stock Exchanges in India", "New Delhi, Thomson Press (India)", "1972"

"Gupta. L.C.", "The Ownership of Industrial Securities in India", "Indian Economic Journal, vol. 13 (Oct-Dec 1963)", "pp. 232-255"

"Heinkel, R.", "A Theory of Credibility: Costless Signals in a Rational Expectations, Infinite Horizon Model", "A Working Paper (University of British columbia,", "Vancouver"

"Hess,P.", "The Ex-Dividend Day Behaviour of Stock Returns: Further Evidence on Tax Effects", "Journal of finance, Vol. 37 (1982)", "pp. 445-456"

"Holt, C.C.", The Influence of Growth Duration on Share Prices", "Journal of Finance, Vol. 42 (Sept. 1962)", "pp. 465-75"

"Jaffe, Lillian H", "A Study of Stock Splits, 1946-56", "Unpublished doctoral dissertation of Graduate School of Business Administration,", "New York, 1957"

"Johnson, J.", "Econometric Methods","New York: McGraw Hill Book Company", "1963"

"Kalay, A.", "The Ex-Dividend Day Behaviour of Stock Prices: A Re-examination of the Clientele Effect", "Journal of Finance, Vol. 37 (1982)", "pp. 1059-1070"

"Kwan, C.", "Efficient Market Tests of the Informational Content of Dividend Announcements: Critique and Extension", "Journal of Financial and Quantitative Analysis, Vol. 16 (1981)", "pp. 193-205"

"Lakonishok, J. and Vermaellen", "Tax Reform and Ex-Dividend Day Behaviour", "Journal of Finance, Vol. 38 (1983)", "pp. 1157-1176"

"Lamoureux, G.C. and Poon, P.", "The Market Reaction to Stock Splits", "The Journal of Finance, Vol. 42 (1987)", "pp. 1347-1370"

"Leland, H. and Pyle, D.", "Informational Asymmetries, Financial structure, and financial intermediation", "Journal of finance, Vol. 32 (1977)", "pp. 371-387"

"Liao, S.S.", "Shareholder Oriented Managers", "Financial Analysts Journal, (1975)", "pp. 62-71"

"Lintner, J.", "The Valuation of Risk Assets and the Selection of Risky Investments in Stock Portfolios and Capital Budgets", "Review of Economics and Statistics, Vol. 47 (Feb. 1965)", "pp. 13-37"

"Lintner, J.", "Distribution of Incomes of Corporations Among Dividends, Retained Earnings and Taxes", "American Economic Review, Vol. 46 (May 1956)", "pp. 97-113"

"Little, I.M.D.", "Higgledy Piggledy Growth", "Bulletin of Oxford Institute of Statistics, November, 1961", "pp. 412"

"Lorie, J.H. and Hamilton, M.T.", "The Stock Market Theories and Evidence", "Homewood, Illinois: Richard D. Irwin, Inc.,", "1973"

"Malkiel, Burton G. and John C. Cragg", "Expectations and the Structure of Share Prices", "American Economic Review, Vol. 60 (Sept 1970)", "pp. 601-617"

"Markowitz, H.", "Porfolio Selection: Efficient Diversification of Investments", "New York: Wiley", "1959"

"Markowitz, H.M.", "Portfolio Selection", "New York: John Wiley and Sons", "1959"

"Marris, R and A. Singh", "A Measure of Firm's Average Share Price", "Journal of Royal Statistical Society, Series A, vol. 129 (1966)", "pp. 74-97"

"Masulis, Ronald W.", "The Effects of Capital Structure Changes on Security Prices: A Study of Exchange Offers", "Journal of Financial Economics, Vol. 8, (1980)", "pp. 139-178"

"Masulis, R.", "Stock repurchase by Tender Offer: An Analysis of the Causes of Common Stock Price Changes", "Journal of Finance, Vol. 35 (1980)", "pp. 305-319"

"Masulis, R.", "The Impact of Capital Structure change on the firm Value: Some Estimates", "Journal of Finance, Vol. 38, (1983)", "pp. 107-126"

"May, G.O.", "Stock Dividends and Concepts of Income", "Journal of Accountancy, October, 1953", "pp. 427-431"

"Michaelsen, J.B.", "The Determinants of Dividend Policies: A Theoritical and Empirical Study", "Unpublished Doctoral Dissertation, Graduate School of Business, Chicago", "1961"

"Miller, M.H. and Modigliani, F.", "Dividend Policy, Growth and the Valuation of Shares", "Journal of Business, Vol. 34 (October 1961)", "pp. 411-433"

"Modigliani, F. and Merton H. Miller", "The Cost of Capital, Corporation Finance and the Theory of Investment", "American Economic Review, Vol. 42 (June 1958)", "pp. 262-97"

"Morgan, E.V., and Taylor, C.", "The Relationship Between Size of Joint Stock Companies and the Yield of their Shares", "Economica, Vol. 34 (October 1966)", "pp. 116-127"

"Mossin, Jan", "Equilibrium in a Capital Asset Market", "Econometrica, vol. 34 (October 1966)", "pp. 768-783"

"National Council For Applied Economic Research", "Capital Markets in a Planned Economy", 1966"

"Nerlove, Marc", "Factors Affecting Difference Among Rates of Return on Investments in Individual Common Stocks", "Review of Economics and Statistics, Vol. 50 (August 1968)", pp. 312-331"

"Ohlson, J. and Penman, S.", "Variance Increases Subsequent to Stock Splits: An Empirical Aberration", "working paper (University of California, Berkeley, CA)", "1984"

"Ojha, P. Raj", "Corporate Dividend Policy in Indian Cotton Textiles Industry", Unpublished Ph.D. Thesis submitted to the University of Rajastan",""

"Pettit, R.", "Dividend Announcements, Security Performance and Capital Market Efficiency", "Journal of Finance, vol. 27 (1972)", "pp. 993-1007"

"Poterba, J.", "Dividends and Taxes: Interpreting Ex-Dividend Evidence", "Working paper (Massachusetts Institute of Technology, Cambridge, MA)", "1982"

"Rayner, A.C. and I.M.D. Little", "Higgledy Piggledy Growth Again", "Oxford: Basic Black-Well", "1966"

"Ross, S.", "The Determination of Financial Structure: The Incentive Signalling Approach", "Bell Journal of Economics, vol. 8 (1977)", "pp. 23-40.

"Schleifer, A.", "Do Demand Curves for Stock Slope Down", "Journal of Finance, Vol. 41 (1986)", "pp. 579-590"

"Schlutz, P.", "Transaction Costs and the Small Firm Effect: A Comment", "Journal of Financial Economics, Vol. 12 (1983)", "pp. 81-88"

"Schwert, G.W.", "Size and Stock Returns and other Empirical Regularities", "Journal of Financial Economics, Vol. 12, (1983)", "pp. 3-12"

"Sharma, J.L., Kennedy, Robert", "A comparative Analysis of Stock Price Behaviour on Bombay, London and New York Stock Exchanges", "Journal of Financial and Quantitative Analysis, Vol. 12 (1977)", "pp. 391-413"

"Sharpe, W.F.,", "Capital Asset Pricing: A Theory of Market Equilibrium under Conditions of Risk", "Journal of Finance, Vol. 19 (September 1964)", "pp. 425-442"

"Sharpe, W.F.", "A Simplified Model for Portfolio Analysis", "Management Science, Vol. 9 (January 1963)", "pp. 277-93"

"Simmons, Richard", "Drafting of Commercial bank loan agreements", "Business Lawyer, Vol. 28 (1972)", "pp. 179-201"

"Smith, K.V. and Eiteman, D.K.", "Essential of Investing", "Irwin", "1974"

"Solomon, E. (ed)", "The Management of Corporate Capital", "New York: the Free Press of Glencoe", "1959"

"Spence, A.M.", "Job Market Signalling", Quarterly Journal of Economics, vol. 87 (1973)", "pp. 355-374"

"Srivastava, S.C.", "Prices dividends and Earnings in India", "Paper presented before the sixth Annual Conference of the Indian Ecometric Society", Dec, 1966"

"Stiglitz, J.E.", "Some Aspects of Taxation of Capital Gains", "National Bureau of Economic Research Working Paper No. 1094", "1983"

"Stoll, H.R. and Whaley, R.E.", "Transaction Costs and the Small Firm Effect", "Journal of Financial Economics, Vol. 12. (1983)", "pp. 57-79"

"Tauchen, G., and Pitts, M.", "The Price Variability Volume Relationship on Speculative Markets,", "Econometrica, Vol. 51 (1983)", "pp. 485-505"

"Taylor W. Foster III and Don Vickrey", "The Information Content of Stock Dividend Announcement", "The Accounting Review, Vol. 53, No. 2", "pp. 360-370"

"Taylor, Basil", "Investment Analysis and Portfolio Management", "London: Elek Books", "1970"

"The New York Stock Exchange", "Individual Shareownership around the World, Second Ed.", ", "1963"

"Van Horne, J.", "Financial Management and Policy", "Prentice Hall", "1968"

"Walter, J.E.", "Dividend Policy and Its Influence on the Value of the Enterprise", "Journal of Finance, Vol. 18 (May 1963)", "pp. 280-291"

"Walter, J.E.", "Dividend Policy and Enterprise Valuation", "Delmont, 1967", "pp. 14-16"

"Watts, R.", "The Information Content of Dividends", "Journal of Business, vol 46 (1973)", "pp. 191-211"

"Weston, Fred J", "A Test of Cost of Capital Propositions", "Southern Economic Journal, Vol. 30 (Oct 1963)", "pp. 105-112"

Weston, J and Brigham, E.", "Managerial Finance, 6th Ed.", "Dryden press, Hinsdale, IL", "1981"

"Wilcox, Edmund B.", "Accounting for Stock Dividends: A Dissent from Current Recommended Practice", "Journal of Accounting, August, 1953", "pp. 176-181"

"Williams, J.B." , "Theory of Investment Value", "Amsterdam: North Holland Publishing Company", "1956"

"Woolridge, R.", "Ex-date Stock Price Adjustment to Stock Dividends: A note", "Journal of Finance, Vol. 38 (1983)", "pp. 247-255"

"Woolridge, R.", "Stock Dividends as Signals,", "Journal of Financial Research Vol. 6 (1983)", "pp. 1-12"

"Woolridge, R. and Chamber, D.", "Reverse splits and Shareholder wealth", "Financial Management, vol. 12, (1983)", "pp. 5-15"

"Young, C.", "Stock Market Prices and Volume of Sales", "Econometrica, Vol. 34 (July 1966)", "pp. 676-685"

Index

THE AUTHOR :

Dr. S.N. Sarma is currently a faculty member, Department of Business Management, Osmania University, Hyderabad. He holds an Intermediate Certificate of ICWAI (Institute of Cost & Works Accountants of India) and is associated with Management Development Programmes. Dr. Sarma has, to his credit, a number of research articles and papers published in leading professional journals.

Contd....